INTO ALL THE WORLD

A basic overview of the New Testament

RICHARD L. ROHRBAUGH

A Griggs Educational Resource

published by
ABINGDON/NASHVILLE

INTO ALL THE WORLD

Calligraphy ..... Larry Eads

Graphics ..... Richard Rohrbaugh

Typesetting ..... Patricia Griggs

Copyright © 1976, GRIGGS EDUCATIONAL SERVICE

All rights reserved. No part of this book may be reproduced in any form without permission in writing from the publishers. For information write Abingdon, Nashville, Tennessee.

ISBN 0-687-19460-1

TABLE OF CONTENTS

Preface	1
Chapter 1...INTO ALL THE WORLD: A Basic Overview of the New Testament	4
I. Getting an Overview	6
A. Contemporary Study of the New Testament	9
B. Getting Started...Tools, Methods, Background	10
C. Historical Background	14
D. The Cultural and Religious Setting of the New Testament	18
Chapter 2...JESUS CHRIST IS LORD	28
I. The Growth of the New Testament Writings	29
A. The New Testament as the Church's Book	29
B. Paul's Mission to the Gentiles	30
C. The Written Gospel	31
D. Later New Testament Writings	33
II. The Collection and Formation of the New Testament Canon	36
Chapter 3...THE ACTS OF THE APOSTLES	39
I. The Acts of the Apostles	40
II. The Historical/Critical Background of Acts	41
III. The Story Acts Tells	44
A. Origins in Jerusalem	44
B. Spread Across Palestine	45
C. Expansion into Asia Minor and Europe	46
D. The Gospel in Rome	49
IV. Issues and Answers	50
For Budding New Testament Scholars/Extra Curricular Activities	52
Chapter 4...LETTERS TO NEW CONGREGATIONS	54
I. Paul's Letters to New Congregations	55
A. Concern for a Struggling New Church- I & II Thessalonians	55
B. Issues of Christian Living - I & II Corinthians	56
C. Clarifying the Christian Message - Galatians, Colossians	59
D. A Letter to Loyal Friends - Philippians	62
II. A "Pauline" Letter for all the Churches - Ephesians	62
Chapter 5...THE GOSPEL ACCORDING TO PAUL	65
I. Romans: Paul's Exposition of the Gospel	66
A. The Circumstances of Writing: An Anticipated Visit	66
B. The Key Question: How is Sinful Humanity to be Accounted Righteous Before God?	66
C. The Thread of Paul's Argument	68
II. The Heart of Paul's Faith	70
Chapter 6...THE SYNOPTIC GOSPELS: PORTRAITS OF JESUS	73
I. The Written Gospel	74
A. From Christ-Event to Written Gospel	74
B. The Gospel and the Gospels	76
II. Studying the Gospels	77
A. The Synoptic Problem	77
B. Tools and Methods for Synoptic Study	79
C. Our Objectives in Studying the Synoptics	81

Chapter 7...THE GOSPEL ACCORDING TO MARK 84
    I. The Gospel According to Mark 85
        A. The Structure of Mark 86
        B. Conflict and Good News 87
        C. The Messiah and the Coming Passion 89
        D. The Passion Narrative 90
        E. Epilogue: The Future Victory 91
    II. The Gospel, According to Mark 91

Chapter 8...THE GOSPEL ACCORDING TO MATTHEW 93
    I. The Gospel According to Matthew 94
        A. The Setting 94
        B. Jesus (Matthew) as Teacher 97
        C. The Coming Kingdom: A Drama in Seven Acts 98
    II. The Gospel, According to Matthew 104

Chapter 9...THE GOSPEL ACCORDING TO LUKE 106
    I. The Gospel According to Luke 107
        A. Salvation History: A Universal Story 109
        B. The Structure and Story of Luke 112
    II. The Gospel, According to Luke 116

APPENDIX TO SYNOPTIC STUDY: The Problem of the Historical Jesus 118

Chapter 10...THE CHURCH AND THE FAITH IN THE WORLD 122
    I. The Church and the Faith in the World 123
        A. Organization and Orthodoxy - I, II Timothy, Titus 123
        B. The Practice of the Faith - James 126
    II. The Gnostic Threat: Heresy and Immorality - Jude, II Peter 129

Chapter 11...THE PERSECUTION OF THE CHURCH 133
    I. The Persecution of the Church 134
    II. Letters of Comfort and Encouragement 135
        A. Suffering for Christ - I Peter 135
        B. The Pioneer and Perfector of Faith - Hebrews 136
        C. He Who Overcomes - Revelation 138

Chapter 12...THE UNIVERSAL GOSPEL 147
    I. The Universal Gospel 148
        A. The Johannine Literature 148
        B. The Letters of John 149
        C. The Gospel According to John 152
    II. The Gospel, According to John 159

APPENDIX I...Where Do We Go From Here in New Testament Study? 162

APPENDIX II... A Summary of New Testament Writings 164

APPENDIX III...The Ultimate "Try This"! 167

PREFACE

It has become commonplace in Protestant churches to deplore the demise of Biblical knowledgeability among both laity and clergy. Wistful sighs for better days in the past when people knew and used their Bibles usually imply that if we somehow could recapture our knowledge of the Scriptures, many of our problems and anxieties would disappear.

Perhaps there is truth in that. Not in the simplistic sense which assumes that mere knowledge of certain facts and phrases will introduce sanity and tranquility, but in the rather more profound sense that a people who have lost touch with their roots also lose their sense of direction. To wrestle with the Scriptures, to allow them to speak to us the word of God's judgement upon the insanity and injustice of the human enterprise, and at the same time to hear in them the renewing word of God's eternal grace, is to make real the dialogue with the living God. Doing so will not in some magical way make our problems disappear, yet countless Christians through the ages have testified that in their dialogue with the Scriptures as a living word, the Spirit of God has begun to blow fresh winds across the landscape.

It is in the hope of contributing to that ongoing process of watching for new signs of the Spirit that this book has been written. Our objective, stated frequently throughout the book, is to gain an overview of the New Testament that can provide a foundation on which to build life-long study. It is an attempt to look at the tree before one focuses in detail on the leaves. While many people in the Church are familiar with isolated parts of Scripture, gaining a grasp of the whole has eluded them and consequently made the parts hard to relate to one another.

Writing an introduction to the New Testament is, of course, nothing new. It has been done countless times by able people with much insight to offer, though some such efforts in the past have naturally gone out of date because of the constant advances in Biblical research. Recent assessments of the Dead Sea Scrolls, for example, have led to a new appreciation of the Hebraic background of New Testament material that was once thought to be Greek in outlook. Our understanding of many of the things Jesus said and did has likewise been altered by recent knowledge of the Essene sect. The unfortunate thing is that so much of the research being done by New Testament scholars filters into the Church very slowly or not at all.

Part of the reason for this is the nature of what has been written in the past to introduce people to the New Testament. Much of it is so technical and scholarly that it is difficult to read, and even more difficult to relate to anyone's life. There is, after all, no point in knowing the technical details for their own sake. Much enriching insight that scholars have produced has bypassed the Churches because it was given to them (and to pastors) in a form that bore little human relevance to everyday life.

At the other extreme have been the many popular introductions to the New Testament that address the real problems of living in today's world, but which bear only small relation to the New Testament. Shallow scholarship has not served the cause of making the New Testament understandable; it has merely impoverished our appreciation for the depth the New Testament has to offer.

A former professor of mine used to say that true simplicity lies on the far side of complexity; on the near side lies simplemindedness. This says it pretty well. What we need in the Church is depth of scholarship on the one hand, and on the other, a way of appropriating that depth in a manner that affects our lives in the real world.

To claim such for the present project would obviously be saying too much. Our intent has been to include sufficient depth of scholarship that we avoid shallow popularization, and yet to do so in a clear and simple way that addresses contemporary life questions. Many important scholarly issues have been set aside in the interests of clarity, but the tools of scholarship have been introduced as a means of mining riches otherwise missed. Charts, maps and diagrams have all been used so as to save the reader from being overwhelmed with words. Above all, the TRY THIS exercises have been included as suggestions for relating the material to the life experience of the readers. Most of these exercises are *inductive* experiences and thus intended to help the reader *sense* the meaning of New Testament concepts rather than be overly analytical about them. These exercises - together with any others one's imagination can produce - are meant to be an integral part of the study, and the place where one asks what it all means for his own life.

It is also important to note that the majority of the inductive exercises are meant to be used with a *group*. The reasons for that are theological as well as practical. While there is nothing wrong with individual Bible study, it is within the Christian community where insights and feelings are *shared* that the Scriptures best come alive. Not only do others provide a check upon our subjectivity, but their care and concern for us as persons can create the kind of community to which these writings were first addressed. Virtually all of the New Testament was written to the Christian community to meet the needs of the group that shared a new life together in Christ.

Though most books have on them the name of an author, most are also the result of much assistance on the part of friends and colleagues. This book is a bit unusual in that regard. Every line, every chart, every chapter of it has been gone over by an editorial group in our congregation. Every TRY THIS has been tried. Many were contributed by members of the group. Others proved unworkable and were changed. Since one of our criteria for producing the book was its usability and readability in an average congregation, it seemed appropriate to allow a congregation to help produce it.

The stamina and resourcefulness of this editorial group has been of the first rank. They met weekly for 20 weeks to go over the material as it was produced, and can rightly take credit for what lies herein. The discipline provided by the weekly deadlines they imposed is beyond doubt the reason this book exists. From them much that is in the book has been learned, and I cannot fail to offer my gratitude to them:

    Dorotha Borland
    Wayne and Stacey Borum
    Margi Brown
    Sharon Holbrook
    Mary Hillgaertner
    Adrian Jordshaugen

    Jean Rutherford
    Margaret Shearer
    Nora Shearer
    David Smith
    Evelyn Tunnell

My special thanks goes to Patty Holt who did all the typing and checking of the manuscript. For these people, the New Testament has become a living book. Our hope is that it will become so for you as well.

St. Mark United Presbyterian Church
Portland, Oregon
June, 1976

Richard L. Rohrbaugh

CHAPTER 1

INTO ALL THE WORLD

A BASIC OVERVIEW OF THE NEW TESTAMENT

Getting involved in the HUMAN situation that occasioned the New Testament will enliven its capacity to speak to us about what GOD is doing in our own lives.

* *

IN THIS CHAPTER WE WILL LOOK AT.....

I. Getting an Overview
    A. Contemporary Study of the New Testament
    B. Getting Started....Tools, Methods, Background
    C. Historical Background
    D. The Religious and Cultural Setting of the New Testament

INTO ALL THE WORLD

A BASIC OVERVIEW OF THE NEW TESTAMENT

The New Testament is the Church's book. Another way of saying that is to acknowledge that the Christian faith did not spring from the New Testament, but the New Testament from the Christian faith. In the earliest years of the Christian movement, there was neither time nor need to write books. The memory of Jesus was still vigorous in the minds of the eyewitnesses, and many expected the return of Christ in their own lifetime. Hence preaching took priority over writing.

When the earliest Christians did write it was initially because situations developed which prompted letters - letters of thanks, criticism, instruction, advice or encouragement. In the later decades of the first century, situations arose which required books - books for detailed instruction in the faith, accounts of Jesus' life, correction of heresies that threatened to sidetrack the Gospel, or accounts of the earliest beginnings of the Christian movement.

The New Testament thus emerged out of very practical and specific situations in which more than the normal oral communication was needed. As we begin our study of the twenty-seven books of the New Testament it will be helpful to try to put ourselves into the world and circumstances of the people for whom a particular book was written. Doing so will help us sense the living worth of the writing. Getting involved with the HUMAN situation that occasioned the New Testament will enliven its capacity to speak to us about what GOD is doing in our lives.

I. GETTING AN OVERVIEW

Our purpose in what follows will be to get an OVERVIEW of the New Testament. Many times in the Church we study short passages or single verses, but fail to see how they fit in the overall picture. This material is designed to help you get the big framework in mind so that later study of the details will prove more rewarding.

This kind of objective (in what follows) will require simplicity - keeping the more obtuse details and technical considerations out of the way in order to gain an overview in outline. Since the New Testament books as we have them are not arranged in chronological order it is difficult for many people to hang them on the story-line of what was happening in the first century A.D. This tends to further confuse the big picture. The format we will be following will use the approximate chronological sequence of the New Testament's production so that you will better be able to grasp how it emerged. This means we will *not* be starting with the Gospels since they were actually written later in the first century. We will start with the Apostolic period and the account of it given in the book of ACTS. As the story of the early church begins to develop, we will introduce the Church's literature in the situations that actually produced it.

Examine the order of the New Testament books. What purpose can you see in this order? If the Gospels were written later than Paul's letters, what reasons might have led the early church to place them first? What does the order tell you about how the books stand in relation to each other?

The chart on the next page will help you get a handle on the 27 New Testament Books....

6

GOSPELS

Matthew
Mark → These three Gospels are called the 'synoptics' because they are so similar they can be read together.
Luke

John

HISTORY

Acts of the Apostles ← Here is the basic 'story-line' for our New Testament study.

PAUL'S LETTERS

Romans
I & II Corinthians
Galatians

Ephesians
Philippians
Colossians
I & II Thessalonians
I & II Timothy
Titus

→ These four letters are 'Pauline', but were not written by Paul himself. They were written by a follower of Paul near the end of the First Century.

Philemon

AN ANONYMOUS LETTER

Hebrews

CATHOLIC (written to the whole church) LETTERS

James
I & II Peter
I, II & III John
Jude

AN APOCALYPSE

Revelation

> Even though the above is the order of the books in our New Testament today, it not the chronological order and is not the order in which we will be studying them. Our purpose is to set each book in the human situation which gave rise to it and that will require a quite different order. The time-line and chart following will show you the order we intend to use in studying the New Testament.

7

NEW TESTAMENT CHRONOLOGY

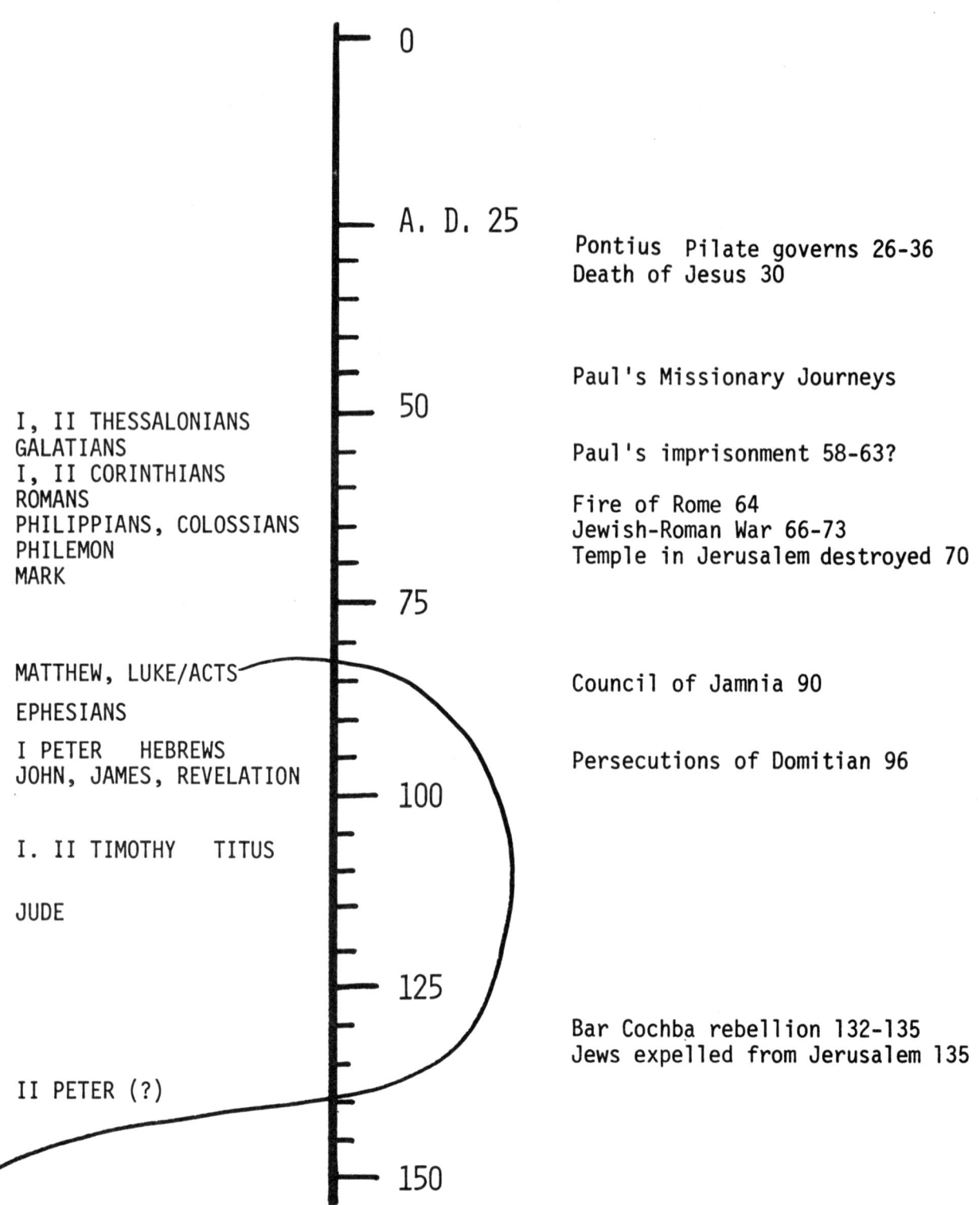

	Pontius Pilate governs 26-36
	Death of Jesus 30
	Paul's Missionary Journeys
I, II THESSALONIANS	
GALATIANS	Paul's imprisonment 58-63?
I, II CORINTHIANS	
ROMANS	Fire of Rome 64
PHILIPPIANS, COLOSSIANS	Jewish-Roman War 66-73
PHILEMON	Temple in Jerusalem destroyed 70
MARK	
MATTHEW, LUKE/ACTS	Council of Jamnia 90
EPHESIANS	
I PETER HEBREWS	Persecutions of Domitian 96
JOHN, JAMES, REVELATION	
I, II TIMOTHY TITUS	
JUDE	
	Bar Cochba rebellion 132-135
	Jews expelled from Jerusalem 135
II PETER (?)	

We plan to "lift" the book of ACTS out of this order and use it as the basis for the chronology on which to locate the other books. Hence we shall study ACTS first even though it was written later.

A. Contemporary Study of the New Testament

Since the New Testament is not really a single book, but a collection of 27 books from a wide variety of authors and circumstances, it reflects human situations which are as varied as those we experience in Christianity today. This means that the New Testament is really a 'living' document that has the capacity to get under your skin. We must know some ancient history in order to understand what the New Testament writers were saying, but it is not history for its own sake we want to know. Our real aim is to hear God speak to us NOW through the Biblical story. For that to really happen we need a mix of important elements that go into any real study of the New Testament:

1. First there is history. We are going to make heavy use of what scholars call the 'historical-critical' method. That is, we are going to learn about authors, audiences, editors, and historical situations out of which the New Testament came. Very quickly in our study we will see why this historical background makes a critical difference in how the New Testament is to be understood.

2. Secondly, we need to consider our Christian tradition. We are not the first Christians to study the Bible, and many before us have drawn rich insights for their eras and lives. Some attempts at understanding the New Testament in the past seem strange to modern ears, others do not. Moreover, there is always the need for a 'fresh' look unspoiled by trite cliches. But still, ways of using and understanding the literature from the past will help us relate the New Testament to our own lives and our own era in new ways.

3. The point of it all, of course, is our own living experience. Our society and its ways of looking at the world are the backdrop over against which *we* must read the New Testament. An important ingredient in this is your own personal set of understandings and experiences, and this you must supply yourself. In a sense, *you* must complete the study of the New Testament today by allowing the interchange it seeks between itself and the reader.

So.....we are going to gear up to study the New Testament for ourselves. As we start, we need to look at some tools and methods.

B. GETTING STARTED... TOOLS, METHODS, BACKGROUND

A NEW TESTAMENT

Obviously we have to start with the New Testament itself. You are probably aware of the many newer translations that are available and may be confused by them. Actually they represent a variety of attempts to use the original language of the New Testament manuscripts and from them produce a translation that is faithful to the text and yet highly readable by modern Americans. Here is a partial list of translations you may want to look at:

1. KING JAMES VERSION

   Still the favorite of many, the KJV was published in the year 1611 by a group of English divines. The Elizabethean English is sometimes foreign to modern ears, and is based on fewer and later manuscripts of the original languages than newer translations.

2. REVISED STANDARD VERSION

   An attempt in 1946 to up-date the KJV on the basis of better manuscript evidence from recent discoveries. Accurate, but not always readable.

3. NEW ENGLISH BIBLE

   Completed in 1970, an excellent translation that is both accurate to our best manuscript evidence and in highly readable English. Occasional British idioms may bother American readers.

4. NEW JERUSALEM BIBLE

   A Roman Catholic translation done in French in 1954, that has been freshly re-worked into English (1966). Both readable and accurate.

5. TODAY'S ENGLISH VERSION (Good News for Modern Man)

   Produced by the American Bible Society for American readers. The Old Testament is scheduled for completion in 1976; the New was finished in 1966. Highly readable, generally accurate and competent. (A few unhappy sections, but that could be said of almost any translation, since bringing ideas from one language into another is *very* difficult and always involves compromise choices of words.)

6. PHILLIPS NEW TESTAMENT (revised 1972 edition)

   More a paraphrase than a translation, but a responsible and sound attempt at this risky business. Extremely readable. Portions of the Old Testament are also coming out.

7. BARCLAY NEW TESTAMENT

   An attempt made by an outstanding British scholar to put the New Testament in modern English. Done in 1969.

Since *all* translations involve the great difficulty of trying to capture the tone and meaning of another language with words that are poor equivalents at best, it is perhaps a good idea for the serious student of the Bible to have available more than one translation. Comparison of several translations can often clarify meanings for the English reader that are otherwise obscure.

One should use paraphrases like that of J. B. Phillips with caution. They are not meant to be translations in the strictest sense, and inevitably involve the bias of the author in attempting to capture the 'sense of the text' rather than a literal translation. While the PHILLIPS NEW TESTAMENT is a highly responsible effort, others are not. The LIVING BIBLE for example, while highly readable and worth using, is of questionable accuracy at many points.

Obtain as many translations of the New Testament as possible. Read several familiar passages in each and compare the style of the various versions. Try reading Matthew 5:1-13, John 1:1-8, I Corinthians 13.

It might be that you will want to use a different version for study than you do for more devotional reading.

There are several tools that will aid your study of the New Testament which you might want to purchase or find in a library. They are not substitutes for reading in the New Testament itself, but they will make it easier to figure out the meaning of what you are reading.

TOOLS FOR BIBLICAL STUDY

A BIBLICAL ATLAS

The New Testament is full of strange names and places. Some time spent getting familiar with the geography of the New Testament world will pay real dividends when you get to reading. It will help if you have several maps you can refer to as you go along.

   An excellent set of maps in handy form for your own study is:
   THE SACRED LAND
   A. J. Holman Company
   East Washington Square
   Philadelphia, Penn. 19105

   Another outstanding atlas is:
   OXFORD BIBLE ATLAS (2nd edition)
   Oxford University Press
   New York 1974
   Cost: Approximately $4.00 (paper)

A BIBLE DICTIONARY

This is an almost indispensible item. It contains alphabetical articles on almost every name, place, idea or event in the Bible. It is a gold-mine of information to help you set the New Testament books in proper historical situations.

For Example: There are seven men named 'Herod' mentioned in the New Testament! Did you ever try to figure out who was whom?

Look up 'Herod' in a Bible Dictionary and it will give you all the detail you need to locate which Herod where.

A good one-volume Bible Dictionary is:
HARPER'S BIBLE DICTIONARY
Harper & Row, Publishers
New York
Cost: Approximately $12.50

One of the best though a bit expensive is:
THE INTERPRETERS BIBLE DICTIONARY (5 volumes)
Abingdon Press
Nashville
Cost: Approximately $85.00

A CONCORDANCE

If you have ever had the frustrating experience of half-remembering a Biblical quote and been unable to find it in the text, you need a concordance. A concordance lists every important New Testament word alphabetically and then gives all the places that word is found.

For example: Let's say you can faintly remember Jesus having said something about 'living by more than bread alone'. However, you cannot find the verse in your New Testament.

With a concordance, you simply look up the word 'bread' and note all the places that word appears in the New Testament. Most concordances list the words in a phrase to help you find what you want:

1.	stones to become loaves of bread	Mt. 4.03
2.	'Man shall not live by bread alone,	4.04
3.	Give us this day our daily bread;	6.11
4.	of you, if his son asks him for bread,	7.09
5.	God and ate the bread of the Presence,	12.04

Hence the one you want is easy to pick out.

A good concordance, made to go with the Revised Standard Version is:
   RSV HANDY CONCORDANCE TO THE BIBLE (paper)
   Zondervan Publishing Co.
   Grand Rapids, Michigan
   Cost: Approximately $1.50

   Also available from:
   Griggs Educational Service
   1731 Barcelona Street
   Livermore, CA 94550

A NEW TESTAMENT COMMENTARY

A tool you might want to consider is a New Testament commentary. There are far too many in print to list here, but each is an attempt to go through the New Testament verse by verse and help you with the meaning. Obviously such interpretations are editorial in nature and hence you may want to consider several to get a wide range of insight. Check with your pastor, church library or public library to borrow a commentary.

HISTORICAL STUDY OF THE NEW TESTAMENT

One of the components of our study of the New Testament will be history - in a very broad sense of that term. We will need to know something of the historical circumstances of the New Testament, its authors, its intended audience, the circumstances that provoked its writing and so on. Before you write off such historical study as of interest only to technical scholars, consider the following example:

   In Matthew chapter 5 the author has collected some of Jesus'
   sayings into what we now call the Sermon on the Mount. Some of
   the sayings give Jesus' re-interpretation of the old Mosaic law.

   Matt: 5:31-32   It was also said (of old), 'Whoever divorces his wife
                   let him give her a certificate of divorce.' But I
                   say to you that every one who divorces his wife, except
                   on the ground of unchastity, makes her an adultress.

How many times have you heard that quotation followed by convoluted reasoning about how a divorced woman today is to be considered an adultress in the eyes of God (or rather, in the eyes of a judgemental Christian!)?

However, when that verse is set in the proper HISTORICAL setting, its meaning comes much clearer:

   - in Palestine in that period women could not work out of
     the home as women do now.
   - a single woman before marriage was in the custody and care
     of her father.
   - a married woman was in the custody and care of her husband.

a divorced woman was in the custody and care of no one, could not work in our sense of the word, and was therefore forced onto the street as a prostitute.

Granted our social customs today are a bit different, but IN THAT SOCIETY Jesus' words were almost literally true - whoever divorced his wife forced her into a life of prostitution!

The point is simple and could be multiplied a thousand times over. When studied in its proper historical setting the Bible comes alive with the richness and flavor of real, authentic human experience!

The method for getting at these questions about history, literary sources, authorship, editorship and so on, is called by scholars the HISTORICAL-CRITICAL METHOD. Its aim is to answer as clearly as possible what the texts meant in their original setting so that we can ask with greater force what they mean to us now.

C. HISTORICAL BACKGROUND

Before we can pick up the story of the emerging church of the first century A.D. we need to understand the background in Palestine that led to the announcement by John the Baptist that the 'Kingdom of God is at hand'.

In the sixth century B.C. the Jewish people had been overrun by the Babylonians and taken captive. We call this the EXILE, and it was a bitter time for those carried away.

Babylonian exile - 597 B.C.

Many of the Jews did not return home to Palestine when the Persians offered them the opportunity in 538 B.C. These Jews, together with many who had fled before the Babylonian conquest, scattered over the Mediterranean World. By the time of Christ, this DIASPORA or DISPERSION out-numbered the Jews living in Palestine.

Persian rule - 538 B.C.

Jewish return to Israel

Dispersion of the Jews

Persian rule lasted until the conquests of Alexander the Great in the year 333 B.C. Alexander's attempt to 'hellenize' (make Greek in culture) his empire was strenuously resisted by many of the Jews in Palestine, but with mixed success. Finally, in the year 165 B.C. Antiochus Epiphanes, the Hellenistic ruler, outlawed Judaism in the attempt to stamp out opposition. His profanation of the temple sparked the Jewish

Conquests of Alexander the Great 333 B.C.

Antiochus outlaws Judaism

uprising known as the MACCABEAN REVOLT which succeeded in bringing political independence to Israel for the first time in 500 years.

Maccabean revolt 165 B.C.

Our OLD TESTAMENT comes to a chronological close with the book of Daniel, a ringing statement of encouragement to the Jewish people to resist Antiochus and look for the coming of the 'Kingdom of God.'

Old Testament closes with book of Daniel

The MACCABEES enjoyed spectacular success for a time, but soon fell to quarreling among themselves. Fierce feuding broke out over the high priesthood, by now both a religious and political office. Finally a citizen's committee for the Jewish people urged Roman support for the high priesthood, with the result that political control passed to the Romans. First Antipater and then Herod (the Great) were appointed Roman vassals and each scrupulously carried out Roman policy.

Maccabean independence 165-63 B.C.

Roman Takeover - 63 B.C.

Roman Vassals rule Palestine

Herod the Great 40-4 B.C.

HEROD THE GREAT was a success as a Roman puppet. He rebuilt the temple in Jerusalem, restored cities in Roman style, and encouraged hellenization. He seemed to have a gift for switching to the right side in each Roman civil war. Under his rule Jerusalem became the pride of the Roman east.

Herod the Great rebuilds Jerusalem and the Temple

Herod was also a bloodthirsty tyrant. He coldly killed his wife and three of his many sons for fear of plots against him, and is reported in Matthew 2:16 to have killed all the male children of Bethlehem at the time of Jesus' birth for the same reason. Jesus was born late in Herod's reign, possibly near 5 B.C. (accounting for modern calendar corrections).

Jesus is born c. 5 B.C.

Jesus' life and ministry took place in Palestine in the first 30 years of the modern era. He died about the year A.D. 30 just outside the city of Jerusalem.

Jesus is crucified A.D. 30

When Herod the Great died in about 4 B.C., his kingdom was divided among three of his sons. ARCHELAUS reigned in Judea, Idumea and Samaria until about A.D. 6 when he was deposed for misrule and replaced by a Roman procurator. The procurator, Pontius Pilate ruled from A.D. 26-36 and hence presided at the trial of Jesus.

Herod's son Archelaus rules until deposed for misrule

Pontius Pilate A.D. 26-36

HEROD ANTIPAS, the second son, ruled Galilee and Perea in the north. He is the Herod under whom Jesus grew to maturity and who beheaded John the Baptist. He ruled until A.D. 39.

Herod Antipas rules Galilee

PHILIP, Herod's third son, ruled the region to the northeast of Galilee in a largely Gentile area and was the only son viewed by his subjects with any affection.

Philip rules northeastern Palestine

HEROD AGRIPPA, a grandson of Herod the Great, ruled Palestine from A.D. 41-44, but after his death the territory reverted to direct Roman rule. For twenty years tensions increased between Roman governors and the Jewish people until open revolt broke out in the year A.D. 66. This JEWISH WAR was a disaster that ended in the utter destruction of Jerusalem and the Temple in the year A.D. 70.

Herod Agrippa A.D. 41-44

Roman Procurators take over

Jewish war A.D. 66-73

Temple destroyed A.D. 70

The destruction of the Jewish state was virtually complete. Political and religious groups were scattered and much of the population dispersed. The PHARISEES, one of the few groups remaining intact after the disaster, formed an academy at Jamnia on the coast and there codified what is now our OLD TESTAMENT.

Council of Jamnia codifies Old Testament A.D. 90

The few remaining Jews in Palestine after the war of A.D. 66-73 made a last desperate attempt to regain their nation in the Bar Cochba rebellion of A.D. 132-135. After their defeat, *no Jewish State existed again until modern times!* Jerusalem became the Roman city Aelia Capitolina and Jews living there were banished.

Bar Cochba revolt A.D. 132-135

Banishment of Jews

By the time of the Bar Cochba rebellion the New Testament as we know it was probably complete. If you will go back to the time-line and listing of the New Testament books in chronological order on page 8 and review it in light of the history you have just read, it will be possible to get an overview of the New Testament in the period out of which it came.

One more little historical outline will help us complete the picture we are trying to sketch. The chart below describes the process at work in the fledgling Christian movement that led to the writing of the New Testament. The dates on the time-line will help integrate this information with the other historical data we have been considering:

a.d. 47 — Paul Begins Mission to Gentiles

As new congregations develop, letters are written to them to encourage, guide, teach. I Thessalonians is probably the first New Testament book written.

a.d. 70 — Christianity Spreads Across Empire, Temple Destroyed, Eyewitnesses Die

As the faith moves from its birthplace and eyewitnesses die off, the need for an account of Jesus' life gives rise to the writing of the Gospels.

a.d. 90 — Council of Jamnia

St. John's Revelation written to encourage persecuted Christians and urge them to stand firm. Catholic letters written to encourage, guide new churches.

a.d. 135 — Bar Cochba Rebellion

Letters written to encourage the faithful to remain firm and hold to the pure faith.

D. The Cultural and Religious Setting of the New Testament

Jesus was a Jew. So were the twelve disciples and most of the other earliest Christians. They did not think of themselves as starting a new religion, but as revitalizing and fulfilling an old one. While from the beginning Jesus and his followers did represent something new and revolutionary, nonetheless the backgrounds of Jesus, of early Christianity, and of the New Testament are all to be found in first century Judaism. It was only in the latter part of the New Testament period that the Church became a predominantly Gentile movement and was heavily influenced by the religion and culture of the Greco-Roman world.

THE JEWISH WORLD

Both Judaism and Christianity are *historical* religions. Crucial to both is the notion that God reveals himself in history - in the real events of real people's lives. Hence the Scriptures are largely accounts of the past: legends, sagas, historical narratives, material for celebrating what God had done for his people. The Old Testament is a vast collection of legal, cultic, devotional and narrative material set in an historical framework. Jewish theology was basically a *story* of what God had done.

Judaism: An historical faith

Judaism was also a religion steeped in tradition. If anything is true of both ancient and modern Jewish practice, it is the keeping of the LAW (Hebrew: TORAH). 'Law' in this case means more than a set of statutes, it is the teaching or tradition that includes history, worship, ethics, and culture. The interpreting and keeping of this tradition was the core of Jewish faith in the time of Jesus.

Law (TORAH): history, worship, ethics, culture

Until its destruction by the Romans in A.D. 70, the TEMPLE in Jerusalem was the focal point of Jewish worship. There sacrifices were offered daily and the festivals of the Jewish year celebrated. The altar and the priesthood were the means of mediation or communication with God. In the performance of sacrifices and the keeping of the great festivals, such as Passover, worship became a part of obedience to the Torah.

Temple: sacrifice and celebration of yearly festivals

For most Jews, even those living in Palestine, the practical center of religious life was the SYNAGOGUE. Synagogue worship bears a greater resemblance to modern Jewish (and to Protestant Christian) worship than to the ancient sacrificial practices of the Temple. Prayer and the reading, interpreting and practice of the Torah were the chief features of Synagogue worship.

Synagogue: reading and interpreting the law

As we will learn later in looking at the New Testament, Jewish worship also contributed to the style and language of Christian services. The PSALMS, often called the 'hymnbook of the second Temple,' are both quoted in the New Testament and used as the pattern for Christian hymns and songs. Jewish literary styles, number symbolism, thought patterns and language were all richly influential as the New Testament began to take written form. The *spoken* language in Jesus' day was ARAMAIC, and even though the New Testament was later written in the market-place Greek of the Gentile world, Aramaic remnants from the oral period before things were written down still remain in our New Testament (Cp. Mark 15:34).

Psalms: hymnbook of the Jewish Temple

Aramaic spoken in Jesus' day

The New Testament written in Greek

JEWISH SECTS

Josephus, a colorful Jewish historian who lived during the New Testament period, tells us that there were four religious parties in first-century Judaism, each of which could be defined by its attitude toward the Torah. The four 'philosophies,' as Josephus calls them, were: Pharisees, Sadducees, Essenes, and Zealots.

PHARISEES

The PHARISEES were legalists, and probably the most influential religious group in Palestine in Jesus' day. The term 'pharisee' meant separatist, and denoted a brotherhood dedicated to full obedience to the ancient law.

Pharisees: separatists

Pharisaism was basically a lay movement and placed great stress on purity of practice in the home and around the table. Interpretation and keeping of the law was such a passion with the Pharisees that they tended to look down on people who neglected their religious duties. After the terrible Roman war of A.D. 66-73 wiped out virtually all religious and political associations among Palestinian Jews,

A lay movement - dedicated to keeping and interpreting the law

it was the Pharisees who re-grouped and kept Judaism alive. They formed a rabbinic council near Jamnia on the coast and there collected and codified the Old Testament as we know it today. Modern Judaism is almost entirely the heir of this pharisaical tradition.

*Old Testament
A.D. 90
Council of Jamnia*

SADDUCEES

The SADDUCEES were the priestly aristocracy. Their origins, like those of the Pharisees, are obscure. The Sadducees were to the Temple what the Pharisees were to the Torah: the keepers of the mysteries. They were the custodians of Temple practice and worship. They were also somewhat conservative and tended to cooperate with the Romans. As men of wealth and position in the establishment, it was in their interest to do so.

*Sadducees: priestly aristocracy
Temple custodians
Roman collaborators*

The Sadducees were theologically more conservative than the Pharisees. They would not accept any of the newer oral or written tradition by which the Pharisees sought to extend the influence of the law into every aspect of life. Hence the Sadducees accepted only the five books of Moses as Scripture. Nor would they countenance such late doctrines as the resurrection from the dead.

Theologically conservative, rejected resurrection, all later tradition

ESSENES

The ESSENES are not mentioned in the New Testament, but are known to us from Josephus and other writers. Their identity has come much clearer since 1947 and the discovery of an Essene monastery near the shore of the Dead Sea. The Essene community existed there in the time of Jesus, but was destroyed by the Romans during the great war (A.D. 68).

Essenes: monks living near the Dead Sea

These monks at Qumran (whose library we now call the Dead Sea Scrolls) were deeply repulsed at what they believed to be the impurity of the Temple and the Jerusalem priesthood. They abhorred the widespread laxity in the keeping of the law. A figure they called the 'Teacher of Righteousness' was apparently the founder of the group and under his influence the Essenes withdrew to the desert. There they practiced a rigorous discipline as they awaited the future purification and vindication of the Temple and the Priesthood.

Temple corruption and religious laxity led Essenes to retreat to Qumran

The Essenes believed this great day of vindication would come as a dramatic struggle between the forces of light and darkness. They were in the desert to prepare (Isa. 40:3). Though early excitement among scholars over the similarity of the Essene movement to what we know of John the Baptist has subsided, still the Essenes remain an important element in the climate of Jesus' time. Like many in Israel they were alternately searching the Scriptures and the heavens for signs of God's coming.

Messianic expectancy

ZEALOTS

Strictly speaking these pious cutthroats did not appear as a specific party until about A.D. 66 when they sparked the disastrous revolt against Rome, but the origins of the ZEALOTS were doubtless in the direct-action groups that had been springing up ever since the Romans took control. At least one (Simon) of Jesus' disciples belonged to these Zealot groups.

Zealots: political revolutionaries

The only Jewish sect to survive the Roman war of A.D. 66-73 was the Pharisees. Their concentration on the law as the distinctive core of Jewish identity gave them a vehicle for the practice of their faith in the face of political disintegration. For all our Christian tendency to ridicule the Pharisees for their overenthusiastic legalism, they represented the progressive and abiding element of Judaism that has survived to our own day.

Jewish Sects in Jesus' Day

Pharisees

- Abhorred Greco-Roman culture (Hellenism)
- Laymen, mostly middle-class
- Progressive
- Scriptures: Torah, Prophets, Oral Tradition and (after Jamnia) the Writings
- Affirmed apocalyptic ideas: resurrection, judgement, divine intervention, New Age, Messiah
- Interpreters and doers of the law

Sadducees

- Friendly to Hellenism
- Priesthood, wealthy aristocrats
- Conservative
- Scripture: Torah only
- Denied apocalyptic ideas
- Custodians of Temple, sacrifice

Essenes

- Monastic community
- Withdrew from impurity of temple and cultic practice
- Awaited cataclysmic finale between forces of light and darkness.
- Studied and interpreted Scriptures (Dead Sea Scrolls)

Zealots

- Political revolutionaries
- Fomented direct action
- Sparked Roman War A.D. 66-73

THE BLAZING HOPE

The Judaism of Jesus' day was characterized not only by the traditions from the past, but by its blazing hope for a new future in the kingdom of God. At one end of the spectrum stood those like the Zealots who looked for a dramatic intervention of God in history to destroy the wicked and re-establish the kingdom of Israel forever. At the other end stood the Sadducees whose security and comfort as the Roman-supporting establishment made them little inclined to want either insurrection or divine cataclysm.

Aside from these extremes, men like the Pharisees stood looking for the 'redemption of Israel' (Cp. Luke 24:21). They were not violent revolutionaries, nor were they passive cooperators with Rome. They sought by the keeping of the law to restore Israel to a condition of God's favor such that divine initiative would usher in the New Age.

The hope of a New Age, a messianic age, was widely shared throughout Judaism in Jesus' time. We call this the *apocalyptic* hope. 'Apocalyptic' is a term used to describe the belief that all of history would be divided into two great ages: the Old Age of injustice and death, and a New Age of God's kingdom in which mercy and justice would emerge. History was believed to be moving toward the culmination of this divine plan for a messianic era in which the nation of Israel would be restored and renewed. While many variations on the messianic theme were current in the first century, so that no unanimity existed on when the Messiah would appear or what he would be like, that such a figure would appear and that he would bring in God's kingdom, was a hope shared by nearly all of Jesus' contemporaries.

A vivid catalyst for this dream of history's consummation was the story and promise of God's dealings with the Jewish people contained in the Old Testament. Virtually every New Testament writer, and indeed Jesus himself, made heavy use of the Old Testament promise that a renewed Israel would be given as....
"...a light to the nations, that my salvation
may reach to the ends of the earth." (Isaiah 49:6)

The Scriptures (which included only the Torah and the Prophets until the time of Jamnia - A.D. 90) were believed by all the New Testament writers to have been fulfilled in the coming of Jesus. He was the fulfillment of all that Israel had hoped for, fought for, and dreamed of throughout the barren years of waiting. John the Baptist's dramatic announcement that the kingdom of God was at hand struck precisely the spark all Israel was waiting to see ignited. The time had come to...."prepare the way of the Lord!"

The Apocalyptic Hope

OLD AGE ──────▶   NEW AGE ──────▶

ALSO CALLED:

Present age
Kingdom of this world
Age of darkness

CHARACTERIZED BY:

war, tyranny
injustice, oppression
religious decadence

God's climactic intervention

ALSO CALLED:

Age to come
Kingdom of God
Eternal life

CHARACTERIZED BY:

reign of God, peace
religious renewal,
justice, coming of Messiah

> On a large, blank sheet of paper, make two columns and
> label one 'Present Age' and the other 'Age to Come.'
> Under the heading 'Present Age,' brainstorm a contemporary
> list of characteristics. Where are the hurts, the
> injustices, the tyrannies of the age in which we live?
> The 'Present Age' is as perennial as the grass, but takes
> its own form in every era.
>
> Down the other column list the characteristics of your hope
> for the future. What do you dream about? Look for?
> (Both for society as a whole and for you personally) What
> would be the shape of the 'New Age' for you?
>
> Now ask yourself: Which 'Present Age' characteristics
> you listed today were true of the Biblical era? Which are
> unique to our day? What about your 'New Age?' Will it ever
> come? Even in small measure? How? When? By the interven-
> tion of God? By human effort? Both? What could it mean
> to call Jesus the Messiah (the One anointed to usher in
> the New Age) today?
>
> Take the time to let individuals in your group express
> their feelings on paper. Any who wish to can then share
> their statements with the group.

THE GRECO-ROMAN WORLD

By the third century before Christ the Hebrew Scriptures had been translated
into the Greek language. Done in Egypt, it was probably to aid diasporan Jews
who had lost the use of the old Hebrew and become assimilated into the Greek-
speaking culture we call Hellenism.

Hellenism followed in the wake of the conquests of Alexander the Great. Although Alexander's political empire did not outlive him, the spread of the Greek language, the Greek ways of thinking, dressing and living all did. Roman armies may have eventually conquered the Mediterranean world, including Greece, but Greek culture conquered Rome and the Roman world.

Among those things which Alexander bequeathed to the ancient Near East was the Greek language. A simple dialect of it, known as the *Koine*, became the universal language of the Mediterranean cities. To Judaism and Christianity this was both a threat and a benefit. It threatened to destroy just those distinctively Hebrew ways of thinking and living that characterized Judaism and cradled Christianity. At the same time, the common tongue made possible the spread of Judaism's influence and Christianity's early missionary preaching. Although the Gospels are probably based in part on older Aramaic sources, the entire New Testament as we have it was written in Koine Greek.

Hellenism: Greek language, thought, culture

Koine Greek: the language of the New Testament

Alexander may have created a world, but Rome became its governor. For half a century before Christ and for nearly half a millenium after, Rome gave the Mediterranean world political stability and unity. We call it the *pax Romana* - the peace of Rome. In the two hundred years of Rome's heyday - from 30 B.C. until A.D. 180 - Christianity was born and emerged as a world religion.

Pax Romana: the peace of Rome

The *pax Romana* meant much besides political stability. Law and order, roads, trade, travel and a sense of *oikoumene* (one world) were all by-products of Roman government. All of it helped make the spread of Christianity possible.

Law and order, roads travel, trade, 'oikoumene'

HELLENISTIC RELIGION AND PHILOSOPHY

Christianity did not originate in a period of religious decline. In fact, the most striking characteristic of the Roman cultural situation was the variety and popularity of religion. Paul, speaking in Athens, saw the picture clearly:

> "Men of Athens, I perceive that in every way you are very religious...." (Acts 17:22)

Tumultuous vitality characterized most of the religions Paul encountered.

Official or TRADITIONAL RELIGION in the Roman world was a combination of elements from old Greek and Roman beliefs. Greek religion had consisted of a variety of local deities, each with a holy place or function. Roman religious cults included gods of hearth and family as well as the deities representing public life and the institutions of city and state. By the time of the Christian era Greek and Roman Gods were thought of as the same gods with different names.

Traditional religion: gods, goddesses cult of city and state

Traditional Roman religion faced strong competition by the time of Paul, most of it from cults of oriental origin. MYSTERY RELIGIONS, about which we know relatively little, captured popular fancy and introduced secret rituals widely believed by early Christians to be a source of immoral pagan conduct.

Mystery religions: secret rituals and mythology

GREEK PHILOSOPHY, with its rationalistic outlook on life and the world, gave many people a basis for understanding both traditional religion and the newer cults in a symbolic style. Stories of gods and goddesses were viewed as allegorical descriptions of great truths about life.

Greek philosophy: symbolic, allegorical interpretations of the old religion

A widespread phenomena in the early Christian era - it is perhaps not quite accurate to call it a religion - was GNOSTICISM. Gnosticism probably had its origins in Persian and Babylonian culture, but nonetheless pervasively influenced the world in which Christianity emerged.

Gnosticism: widely influenced early Christianity

Gnosticism involved a deep sense of alienation from the world, particularly the material world and the physical body. Gnostics believed that the immortal soul, imprisoned in this vale of tears, seeks enlightenment (from Gnosis: knowledge) by which the secrets of one's way back to the heavenly home are revealed. The conflict between Christianity and this other-worldly outlook is evident in much of the New Testament.

Alienation from material world, physical body

Salvation by 'secret knowledge'

The variety of religion in the empire was so great that we cannot deal with it all in detail. Astrology fate, magic, hero cults, healing spas and emperor worship were all widespread. It was indeed a very religious world.

Fantastic variety of religious belief

The world in which Christianity emerged was a *religious* world. It was chaotic, complex, vigorous. The question might be raised about how it compares with the world in which we are now trying to read the New Testament.

Either individually or as a group, collect a pile of magazines, newspapers, posters - anything with lots of pictures. Make a collage that captures the religious tone (or lack thereof) of our era as compared to that of the New Testament. If your group does this, all could contribute and then discuss the results. You could share together how you feel about studying the New Testament over against the type of society you have depicted.

The collage might even be kept around as a constant reminder that you are reading the New Testament in a world substantially different in some ways and similar in others to the world in which the New Testament was written.

CHAPTER 2

Christianity did not spring from the New Testament, but the New Testament from Christianity.

* *

IN THIS CHAPTER WE WILL LOOK AT....

I. The Growth of the New Testament Writings
   A. The New Testament as the Church's Book
   B. Paul's Mission to the Gentiles
   C. The Written Gospel
   D. Later New Testament Writings

II. Collection and Formation of the Canon

I. The Growth of the New Testament Writings

The New Testament is obviously not a single book, but a collection of 27 writings put together at different times, by different people, under widely different circumstances. Since our purpose is to gain an overview of this collection in its entirety, a word about the scope and variety of what it contains is in order.

A. The New Testament as the Church's Book

We have already mentioned the fact that the New Testament did not produce the Church; it was the other way around. The importance of this fact will become clearer as we see the variety of literature the New Testament contains and the conditions that gave rise to its writing.

Everything began, of course, with the events of Jesus' life, ministry, death and resurrection. Those events, not the written record of them, brought the small Christian Community into being. Only later did conditions arise which prompted this community to commit its memory of Jesus to the written page.

The 'Christ-event' began the new community

For nearly twenty years the accounts of Jesus remained in oral form. Since no stenographers were present to record Jesus' sayings verbatim, people had to remember them. They shared them with each other by word of mouth. Because most of the people could not read and write anyway, the practice of preserving valued material by memorization was much more common than it is today. And more accurate too. It had to be, since it was the only option available for the majority.

Oral tradition: saving the tradition in living memories

The ORAL TRADITION, as we call it, doubtless contained much about the life and ministry of Jesus that would be fascinating to know, that is now long lost. At first there seemed no real reason to write it all down. The earliest Christians expected the return of Christ in their lifetime, and thus saw no value in written records. It was only a delay in Jesus' return, together with the increasing geographical scope of the Church, that eventually changed the situation.

At first there was little reason to write things down.

Delay of Jesus' return changed things

Gradually small collections of written materials about Jesus came into being. For example, the story of the crucifixion apparently circulated in independent written form for some time before being included in the Gospels. Collections of

29

Jesus' sayings, such as the one in Matthew, chapters 5-7 (we call this the Sermon on the Mount), may have been written as well.

Small written collections began to take shape

As Christianity spread and developed centers of activity outside Jerusalem - in Caesarea and then Antioch - the need to educate new converts speeded up this process of collection. Local needs varied so that some parts of the emerging Church saved stories that would have been less important to other areas. Thus differing collections developed over a period of time. In Acts 18:24 ff. we are told of a fellow named Apollos who came to Ephesus from Alexandria and began to preach. Two Christians in Ephesus, Priscilla and Aquilla by name, immediately recognized there was much about Jesus that Apollos had not heard. So they filled him in.

Needs of local churches shaped the collection process

Different parts of the church knew different traditions

This kind of information-exchange between sections of the Church holding partial accounts of Jesus' life undoubtedly occurred with some frequency. Major Christian centers soon developed local traditions all their own. As time went on the pressure to bring some order to the oral tradition by getting it into writing began to increase. This was the result of a number of factors we shall look at in a minute, but first we must bring along another part of the story.

B. Paul's Mission to the Gentiles

The book of ACTS tells the story of the expansion of Christianity beyond the small beginning in Jerusalem. Caesarea, down on the coast of Palestine, soon became an active Christian center. So also did the region to the north and east of Galilee - the area known as Decapolis (meaning the *ten cities* in Greek). Most of the early converts were Jews who began to see Jesus as their Messiah.

Before long the universal implications of the Gospel created pressure to move into the Gentile world. That mission became the special task and achievement of the Apostle Paul. He began to travel the Mediterranean world, going first into Synagogues among Jews of the Diaspora, and then, from the small nucleus gathered there, into surrounding gentile communities. All along Paul's itinerary new congregations of Christians emerged.

Paul's mission to the Gentiles

Emerging new congregations

Since Paul was a man on the move, he usually left to others the work of cultivating and nurturing what he had begun. In some of the congregations Paul started he probably worked no more than a few months, while in others he may have stayed as long as two years. Wherever Paul traveled he always attempted to maintain his relationships with congregations planted earlier. He sent them letters, often carried by the hand of Christians who had come to visit with messages or questions from these former congregations. Paul also wrote to congregations he himself had not started, but with which he had become acquainted through mutual friends.

Letter-writing maintained contact with the churches

These letters of Paul, written to answer questions, to give advice, or to provide instruction in the faith, were the first literature to be written and saved in our New Testament. Most of the letters are practical and were written to speak to specific needs that arose within the churches, as well as to defend Paul's authority and integrity within the emerging congregations. The letters show a curious lack of interest in the facts of Jesus' life and ministry, concentrating instead on the theological meaning of Jesus' death and resurrection. They begin with the two letters to the Thessalonians, written near A.D. 51 or 52, and close with Philippians, Philemon and perhaps Colossians, written while Paul was under arrest in Rome (A.D. 62-64).

Paul's letters are the oldest literature in our New Testament

I and II Thessalonians came first - A.D. 51-52

Paul almost certainly wrote letters that are lost to us. Several of the letters we do have (such as II Corinthians) are probably editorial compilations of several Pauline compositions. Other letters, written under Paul's name but not actually written by him (we will explain more of this phenomenon later), also circulated among the congregations. All of this activity was intensely practical, meant to meet the day-to-day needs of emerging congregations.

Some Pauline letters now lost

Paul addressed the day-to-day needs of congregations

C. THE WRITTEN GOSPEL

Against the backdrop of these newly developing congregations, we can now pick up our story of these factors that prompted the writing down of the oral tradition about the life and death of Jesus. With the destruction of the Temple of Jerusalem in the year A.D. 70 (an event in the Jewish war A.D. 66-73), and the growing animosity between Jews and Christians, the center of Christian activity began slowly to move away from Jerusalem and Palestine toward the great cities of the Roman empire: Antioch, Ephesus, Alexandria, and Rome itself. It was during this period that the first of our Gospels was written.

The writing of the first Gospel (Mark) was probably not a casual affair. Well into the second century we read of a Bishop named Papias who, though he knew of the existence of written Gospels, preferred the "living tradition" of the Lord to the "content of books." To Papias, Jesus was a living Lord and likewise the tradition about him was alive and developing. Writing down and thus fixing the tradition was probably only done as the result of pressing needs on the part of the Church.

Mark was written first

Some preferred the 'living Gospel' to written books

One obvious reason for written Gospels was the death of eye-witnesses. With those who could speak first-hand dying off, the tradition was in danger. Our Gospel of Mark probably originated in the mid-sixties of the first century as a direct result of the deaths of Peter, Paul, and other apostles in the persecutions of Emperor Nero.

Deaths of eye-witnesses, persecution prompted writing

Other motives prompted written Gospels as well. A Church facing persecution needed to know how Jesus faced death. The relation of Christianity to the law and practice of Judaism had to be clarified.* As Christianity spread to the Gentile (non-Jewish) world, a crisis developed out of the difficulty of relating a religion that was basically Hebrew in outlook to a culture that was Hellenistic. It became a question of communicating the faith to the Gentiles without losing the original character that derived from Jesus, Judaism and Palestine.

The growing need for clarifying the faith prompted questions about Jesus

Standing over all these probable reasons for committing the Gospel to writing was the delay of Christ's return (We call this expected event the *Parousia* a Greek word meaning 'appearance'). Christians kept waiting, but it did not materialize. If life was thus going to go on for a long time attitudes and plans had to be revised. The Church would have to prepare for being here long after the oral tradition was gone. Moreover, if it was going to be necessary to live in the world as Christ's followers for a long time to come, it would be important to know how Jesus had taught his disciples to act.

Delay of the Parousia made written Gospels necessary - to guide the church

As new converts flocked into the churches from the Gentile world, they created another need. They knew little of Jewish tradition, of the Old Testament

---

* *The relationship of emerging Christianity to Judaism, and the transition from one to the other, will be discussed at length in the next chapter.*

or the messianic promise, and thus needed instruction. Materials had to be developed to help them along. The Gospel of Matthew was possibly occasioned by just such a need for instructional material.

New converts needed instruction

The Gospels, then, were the direct result of the needs of the emerging Church. They were written much later than Paul's letters, but were placed first in our New Testament because they were first in importance, not because of their date of composition.

The needs of the church created the Gospels

D. LATER NEW TESTAMENT WRITINGS

By the end of the first century of our era, Christianity had spread across much of the Mediterranean world. The letters of Paul had begun to circulate as helpful, if not yet canonical, material. Other Christian writing had also begun to appear, and it too was occasioned by the needs of the Church.

Sharp controversy quickly followed the establishment of the new churches. Local customs and traditions began to give the Church a varied complexion. Pagan religion and Greek philosophy began to distort things, and persecution drove many would-be converts away. As the churches began to grow and multiply, problems emerged in organizing for the tasks at hand. All of this occasioned literature that is now in our New Testament.

Later writings faced new problems: conflict with pagan culture, Greek philosophy, church structure and organization.

Some of this later writing was an attempt to combat heresy. 'Heresy' is not a term that resonates well in modern ears, but it simply referred to distortions in the faith created by the influence of Hellenistic culture, pagan religion, and the bewildering variety of religious philosophies. Just as Paul had helped the emerging Church clarify its relation to Judaism, so later Christian writers sought to do so in relation to Greco-Roman culture and religion. Letters such as those of John and Jude were occasioned by this crisis.

Heresy - distortions of the faith - occasioned several N. T. letters

Other letters, such as those to Timothy and Titus, were prompted by the need for order in the growing Church. These letters, written in Paul's name, were addressed to young pastors to provide practical help in structuring their congregations for the task of mission. As such they provided helpful advice to all young congregations and for this reason began to circulate. Their later inclusion in the New Testament is obvious testimony to the widespread nature of the problems they address.

The letters to Timothy and Titus address issues of Church order

The last book in our New Testament, the Revelation to John, is one that has long fascinated and confused Christian readers. Sometimes called the Apocalypse (from a Greek word meaning 'vision'), this book was written in symbols and figures of speech that strike the modern reader as utter gobbledygook. Yet most of the symbolism is taken directly from the Old Testament and would have been readily understood by the original readers. The book is a ringing call to stand fast in the face of Roman persecution and to resist to the end the Roman empire's (and Emperor Domitian's) claim to divinity.

The Revelation to John: a call to serve God rather than Caesar

While we will be looking at each of the major sections of the New Testament in more detail as our story begins to unfold, for now it is important to see the bigger picture.* We need a good grounding in the sweep of events and conditions that caused the New Testament to emerge. When this is clear, it is obvious why we are going to start our study of the New Testament with the letters of Paul rather than the Gospels. It may also be clear that the New Testament is not a book of religious theories - it emerged out of the actual life-experience and needs of Christian congregations. If you can grasp this last notion, you will have a handle on the single most important insight in New Testament study!

* *The chart on the next page is designed to help you with the overview problem. Refer to it often!*

GROWTH OF THE NEW TESTAMENT WRITINGS

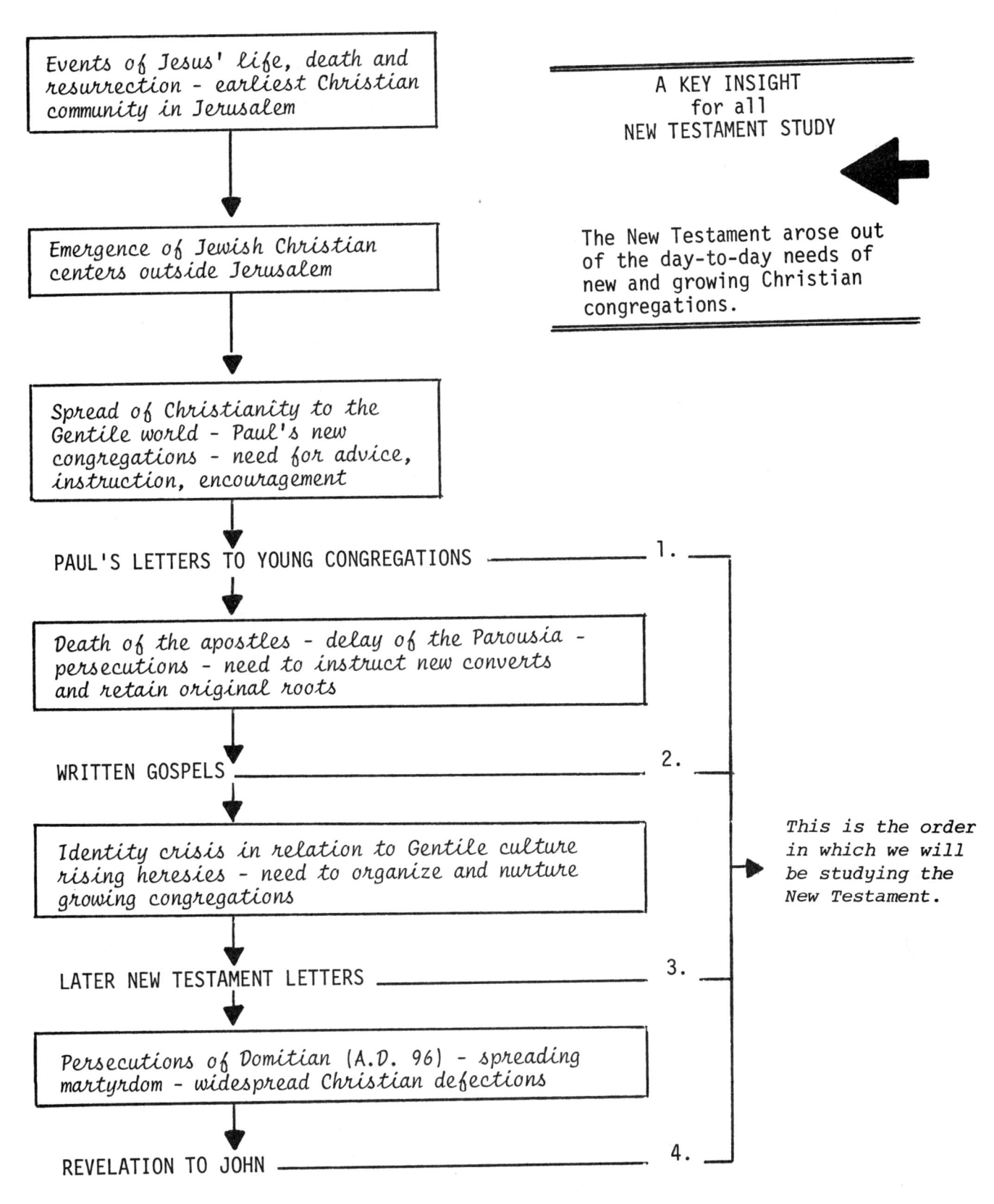

```
┌─────────────────────────────────┐
│ Events of Jesus' life, death and │
│ resurrection - earliest Christian│
│ community in Jerusalem           │
└─────────────────────────────────┘
               ↓
┌─────────────────────────────────┐
│ Emergence of Jewish Christian    │
│ centers outside Jerusalem        │
└─────────────────────────────────┘
               ↓
┌─────────────────────────────────┐
│ Spread of Christianity to the    │
│ Gentile world - Paul's new       │
│ congregations - need for advice, │
│ instruction, encouragement       │
└─────────────────────────────────┘
               ↓
PAUL'S LETTERS TO YOUNG CONGREGATIONS ───────── 1.
               ↓
┌─────────────────────────────────┐
│ Death of the apostles - delay of the Parousia - │
│ persecutions - need to instruct new converts    │
│ and retain original roots                       │
└─────────────────────────────────┘
               ↓
WRITTEN GOSPELS ───────────────────────────── 2.
               ↓
┌─────────────────────────────────┐
│ Identity crisis in relation to Gentile culture  │
│ rising heresies - need to organize and nurture  │
│ growing congregations                           │
└─────────────────────────────────┘
               ↓
LATER NEW TESTAMENT LETTERS ───────────────── 3.
               ↓
┌─────────────────────────────────┐
│ Persecutions of Domitian (A.D. 96) - spreading  │
│ martyrdom - widespread Christian defections     │
└─────────────────────────────────┘
               ↓
REVELATION TO JOHN ────────────────────────── 4.
```

A KEY INSIGHT for all NEW TESTAMENT STUDY ⬅

The New Testament arose out of the day-to-day needs of new and growing Christian congregations.

This is the order in which we will be studying the New Testament.

35

II. The Collection and Formation of the New Testament Canon

Two very approximate dates are important for understanding the development of the New Testament Canon (list of authoritative books - from a Greek word meaning 'rule' or 'norm'):

<u>End of the first century</u>: Most of the books now in the New Testament had been written

<u>End of the second century</u>: Most of our New Testament books were widely recognized as authoritative for the Church

The collection of a Canon which could be regarded as holy Scripture was a process that spanned the second century. While disagreements lasted long after this time, a broad consensus did develop during this period and the roots of that consensus can be found in the circumstances that generated the writings in the first place.

During the period of the New Testament's actual writing, a variety of Christian writings were sifted and collected by congregations in many localities. Some writings were gradually eliminated because they were not the work of apostles or writers with apostolic sources. Others fell into disuse because they lacked value or were considered unsound. By the end of the second century a broad consensus had developed that included about 20 of our 27 books.

The letters of Paul probably began to circulate in his own lifetime and at his own direction (see Colossians 4:16). There is some evidence that Ephesians was a general letter, perhaps written by a disciple of Paul, providing an introduction to a collection of ten of Paul's letters. While not all sections of the early Church agreed on which letters were actually written by Paul, it is probable that shortly after the end of the first century the majority of the Pauline collection was widely known among the churches.

The collection of the four Gospels is shrouded in mystery. By the middle of the second century all four were known to parts of the Church, while in other areas only one Gospel was used. Late in the second century a Christian writer named Irenaeus made an issue of the necessity of four Gospels, almost as if he were writing to people who thought one or the other sufficient.

Several books were slow in gaining consensus recognition. Hebrews was suspect because its authorship was in doubt, and was only finally accepted because it came to be believed that Paul wrote it. Similarly, some sections of the Church did not use Revelation until it was finally accepted as the work of the Apostle John.

Throughout this long process other Christian writings, including other Gospels, fell by the wayside. Some we know of only because they are quoted in writings that have survived. Others, such as the Gospel of Thomas (a recent find at Nag Hammadi in Egypt), have come to light at the hands of modern archaeologists. Though it was not until late in the fourth century that a final list of 27 books was agreed upon, by the year A.D. 200 only minor differences existed among Christians on what should be the rule for the Church.

Two Key Dates......

END OF THE FIRST CENTURY
- Most of our present New Testament had been written

END OF THE SECOND CENTURY
- Most of our present New Testament books were recognized as authoritative for the whole church.

TRY THIS

If you are working at this New Testament study as a part of a group, take a few minutes and try this exercise:

1. Divide the group into the following smaller sections:

   New converts - new Christians, mostly Gentile, with almost no background in the faith, and yet a strong desire to learn in anticipation of soon being baptized.

   Pastors and teachers - people charged with the responsibility for nurturing new congregations and new converts.

   Church administrators - elders and deacons given the task of governing new congregations and organizing them for mission.

   Allow each small group a few minutes to explore the implications of their role in the Church.

2. Give each group a large piece of paper and a felt pen with which to record one or two word answers to the following questions. Let these questions refer *to your present congregation*, not the early Church:

   - What do *we* need to know to fill our role in the Church?
   - What do we want *others* to know about us?
   - What special problems do we have as a group?
   - Where are the points of conflict between us and the non-Christian culture?
   - Do we have needs unique to our congregation?
   - Who in our group is trusted and capable of writing what we need?

3. Let each small group report to the whole suggesting what kind of literature is needed in *your* canon.

   - Letters? From whom? On what subjects?
   - Gospels? Bringing the life of Jesus to bear on what issues?

> - Manuals?
> - Educational resources?
>
> Perhaps these written resources already exist in your congregation. By what process is this material collected and sifted?
>
> 4. Finally, let the group discuss the possibilities for using the New Testament as such a source-book of needed materials. Can anyone in the group identify particular New Testament books that speak to the needs of the small groups?
>
> The exercise is designed to help you gain a feel for the practical circumstances out of which the New Testament canon developed.

This brings us to the close of our introductory material aimed at providing a broad general background for New Testament study. Obviously it has been simplified to the barest outline in the interests of gaining the overview we are after. Those wishing more detail on the New Testament period should consult any of the fine New Testament introductory volumes available today. Here is a list of several good ones:

1. ANATOMY OF THE NEW TESTAMENT by D. A. Spivey and D. M. Smith.
   (New York: MacMillan Publishing Co., 1974.)

2. UNDERSTANDING THE NEW TESTAMENT by H. C. Kee, F. W. Young and K. Froelich.
   (Englewood Cliffs, N.J.: Prentice-Hall, 1973.)

3. THE BIRTH OF THE NEW TESTAMENT by C. F. D. Moule.
   (New York: Harper and Row, 1962.)

4. UNDERSTANDING THE NEW TESTAMENT Edited by Jessie O. Lace.
   (Cambridge: The University Press, 1965.)
   (This is the introductory volume to the New Cambridge Bible Commentary on the New English Bible.)

CHAPTER 3

THE ACTS OF THE APOSTLES

JERUSALEM

ROME

The critical moment for the origin of the Christian Church may be evoked by asking the question, "How did the proclaimer (Jesus) become the proclaimed?"

* *

IN THIS CHAPTER WE WILL LOOK AT....

I. The Acts of the Apostles

II. The Historical/Critical Background of Acts

III. The Story ACTS Tells
    A. Origins of the Church in Jerusalem
    B. Spread throughout Palestine
    C. Expansion into Asia Minor and Europe
    D. The Gospel in Rome

IV. Issues and Answers - The First Pauline Letters

I. THE ACTS OF THE APOSTLES

It has often been said that Jesus came announcing the kingdom of God, but the early Church is what appeared! It has always been a matter of intense interest to Christians to discover how that transition occurred.

Another way to put the matter is this: How did the proclaimer (Jesus) become the proclaimed? That is, how did Jesus, who came proclaiming the kingdom of God to be at hand, become himself the object of the Church's preaching? The story of that remarkable transformation is told for us in the New Testament book called the ACTS OF THE APOSTLES.

"Acts" is a most appropriate title. The story is one of action, and is filled with the excitement, chaos, danger and courage that color the story of Christianity's expansion from Jerusalem to Rome. It can be read even today as an adventure that ranks with the best.

SOME PRELIMINARY NOTES:

As we begin our study of the actual New Testament writings, a few preliminary notes are in order:

1. There is *no substitute for reading the New Testament itself*. We will not get very far if the reader confines his efforts to this book and neglects the New Testament.

2. Since it is an overview of the New Testament we are after, we will not be dealing with specific New Testament passages in great detail. Instead, you will be asked to read sections that will help you to follow the larger picture. An *appendix* at the back of this volume will give you help in dealing with *specific passages* after our overview is complete

3. For each New Testament book to which you will be introduced, you will be given some *background material* - historical/critical information - to help you locate the book in its proper life-situation. It will be helpful to read this material carefully before you attempt to read the New Testament book itself.

4. Since the New Testament uses many names and places with which we are unfamiliar, it will simplify keeping track of things if you always *have a map handy* when you are reading. This will be especially true in our study of the book of ACTS.

5. Reading the New Testament is not merely an exercise in historical curiosity. It means to affect our lives now. Thus your appreciation for what it is attempting to say *to you* will be enhanced if you let your imagination project you into the life-situation of the characters and authors. If you do, you will not only learn more, you will enjoy doing it.

II. THE HISTORICAL/CRITICAL BACKGROUND OF ACTS

The book of ACTS was written by Luke, the author of our third Gospel, probably in the last two decades of the first century (A.D. 80-100). The book begins with the departure of Jesus and the origins of the Church in Jerusalem, and ends with Paul debating and preaching under house-arrest in Rome. It is thus the years of the emerging Church (A.D. 30-60) that the book chronicles.

Traditional author: Luke (who also wrote our 3rd Gospel)

Date: A.D. 80-100

If you will compare Acts 1:1-2 with Luke 1:1-4, you will sense the situation. Luke has written his first volume (the Gospel) to tell the story of Jesus, and his second (Acts) to tell the story of the Church. Both are written to a Theophilus (lover of God) who is probably representative of all Gentile Christians.

Audience: "Theophilus" (Lover of God) All Gentile Christians?

LUKE-ACTS is often called a first-century Christian apology (defense of the faith). Both volumes reflect Luke's concern to show Jesus and Christianity innocent of the widespread charges of subversion toward Rome. This suggests an origin for the Gospel in Rome late in the first century, though our evidence is too slim to pin down these items with certainty.

Purpose: to defend Christianity before the Gentile world

Because Luke collected and used previously written sources in composing his Gospel, scholars believe he probably did the same thing in writing ACTS. But where did this material come from? Did Paul keep a diary of his travels? Did someone record the sermons of Stephen and Peter? Where would Luke have picked up the brief vignettes in 3:1-10 and 5:1-11? How much of the story did Luke witness for himself?

Luke's sources: Paul's diary? eyewitness accounts? sermons?

A comparison of Acts with the letters of Paul reveals a few discrepancies, but in general the details in Acts that can be checked by archaeologists and historians are remarkably accurate. As much as Luke tells us, however, there is much more we would like to know. Did Luke not know how Christianity came to Rome? It is already there when Paul arrives. If he did know, why doesn't he tell us? Also, why is he silent about Paul's death? Since the book was almost certainly written several decades after Paul died, Luke's silence is a mystery.

Unanswered questions:

How did Christianity come to Rome?

How and When did Paul die?

41

In general, Luke's purpose is to explain to the Gentile reader how Christianity spread from Jerusalem to Rome. He justifies the mission to the Gentiles and defends the faith against charges of treason. He provides any "Lover of God" in the late first century with a positive, triumphant account of the crucial origins of the Christian Church.

Luke's purpose: to tell the story of the origins of the Church.

➡️ *The map on the next page will help you keep straight some of the place names we have been talking about. A few minutes spent looking it over will make things easier as we go along.*

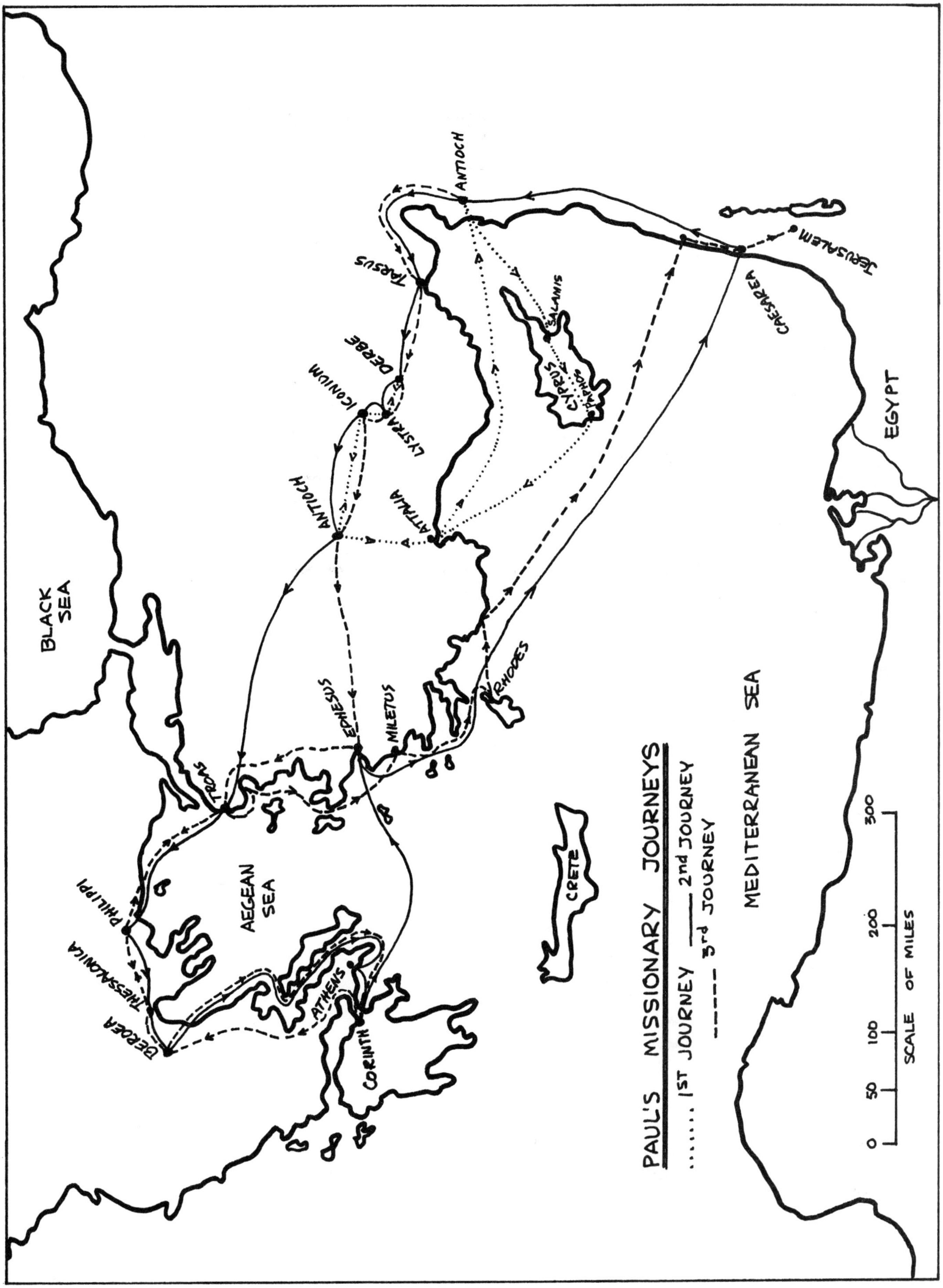
PAUL'S MISSIONARY JOURNEYS
1ST JOURNEY
2nd JOURNEY
3rd JOURNEY
MEDITERRANEAN SEA
SCALE OF MILES
0
50
100
200
300
BLACK SEA
AEGEAN SEA
CRETE
EGYPT
ANTIOCH
TARSUS
DERBE
ICONIUM
LYSTRA
ANTIOCH
ATTALIA
SALAMIS
CYPRUS
PAPHOS
CAESAREA
JERUSALEM
RHODES
MILETUS
EPHESUS
TROAS
PHILIPPI
THESSALONICA
BEROEA
ATHENS
CORINTH

III. THE STORY ACTS TELLS

'From Jerusalem to Rome' is the way the story in Acts has often been described. The characterization is a good one. The turbulent, danger-filled account of Christianity's emergence in Jerusalem and spread across the Roman empire is what Acts is all about.

> To aid in our overview approach, here is a simple outline of the entire book of Acts that will help you grasp what is going on:
>
> | | | |
> |---|---|---|
> | I. | Origins in Jerusalem | Chapters: 1-2 |
> | II. | Spread throughout Palestine | 3-12 |
> | III. | Expansion into Asia Minor and Europe | 13-21 |
> | IV. | The Gospel in Rome | 21-28 |

Before you go further it might help to mark these divisions in the margin of your own Bible for future reference.

It will help if you read Acts 1:1-8 right now:

Note verse 8: "You shall be my witness in ...

    A. _____→ Jerusalem,
    B. _____┌→ Judea,
                   └→ Samaria,
    C.,D. _____, and to the end of the earth."

Here, in simple terms, is the outline of the book!

A. ORIGINS IN JERUSALEM
READ: CHAPTERS 1-2 OF ACTS

The book of ACTS opens with the story of Jesus' departure from the disciples on the Mount of Olives. There Jesus gives the disciples the missionary charge of which the rest of the book will be an account. Matthias is chosen to replace Judas Iscariot so that all will understand the continuity between what God had done in the twelve tribes of Israel and what he was about to do in the 'new Israel' the apostolic mission was creating.

Jesus' ascension

The missionary task of the church

Matthais replaces Judas Iscariot

The apostolic proclamation of the Good News about
Jesus began at PENTECOST. This strange story,
which has been celebrated through much of the Church's
history, clearly locates the origin of the Church
in the coming of the Holy Spirit. The strange   *Pentecost: the gift*
tongues (note that they are not gibberish, but   *of the Holy Spirit*
recognizable languages) are the gift of the
Spirit by which the Gospel is communicated.

PETER'S SERMON at Pentecost, recorded in Acts 2:14-36,   *The first Christian*
is the first account we have of what the preaching   *sermon*
of the apostles was like.

Pentecost represents the initial in-gathering of
new converts into the Church. Most of them would
have been Jews or 'God-fearers' (Gentiles much   *The first Christian*
attracted to Judaism who did not practice all of   *converts*
the ancient law).

Luke concludes this opening section with a fascinating, yet tantalizingly brief, glimpse of the life
of the early Jerusalem Church (2:43-47). It is
clear from his comment about attending the Temple   *Life in the early*
that these first Christians still thought of   *Jerusalem church*
themselves as practicing Jews rather than
adherents of a new religion.

B. SPREAD ACROSS PALESTINE

READ: ACTS 6:1-7:60
             9:1-22
             10:1-11:30

Chapters 3-5 of Acts tell of episodes in the
ministry of the apostles in and around Jerusalem.
Peter and John heal a lame man, speak to the crowd   *The Gospel in and*
about Jesus, and thus provoke the ire of the Jewish   *around Jerusalem*
authorities who forbid them to speak any longer in
Jesus' name.

The story of STEPHEN is told in chapters 6-7 (which   *The stoning of Stephen*
you have been asked to read). Here Luke identifies
for us the sources of the later animosity between   *Animosity between*
Christians and Jews that resulted in their eventual *Christians and Jews.*
split. (Note here Luke's characteristic tendency
to blame the Jews for Jesus' death - not so much
because of antisemitism, but to remove a potential   *Luke's reason for blaming*
cause of trouble between Christianity and Luke's   *Jesus' death on the Jews*
Gentile readers. They would be offended at the notion
that their culture was responsible. Luke's purpose

45

was to defend Christianity before Roman fears of tension and subversion.) As you read the story in Acts, note the irony that the one holding the coats of those who stone Stephen is the young Saul, persecutor of the Church, who later became its greatest Apostle.

Following the stoning of Stephen the second phase of the Church's expansion began. Philip made converts in Samaria, and later on the road from Jerusalem to Egypt converted an Ethiopian. The faith began to spread in an expanding circle beyond Palestine and into the Gentile world. Before we get into that, however, the story of Saul's conversion must be told, since it was Saul (Paul) who became the great missionary to the Gentile world. *Christianity spread across Palestine*

The story of Saul's dramatic conversion is told three times in the book of Acts (in chapters 9, 22, and 26). Read the three stories and try to sense the pivotal role this episode has had in the history of the Church. From here the whole focus of the story begins to shift away from Palestine and toward the mission to the Gentiles. It is a story that climaxes in the heart of the empire: Rome. *The conversion of Saul (later "Paul")*

The account of the visions of Peter and Cornelius (a Roman officer) and the subsequent furor they caused in the Jerusalem Church should not be passed over lightly. Here is a key part of Luke's justification for the Gospel being preached to Gentiles. As Peter says:
  "If then God gave the same gift to them (the Gentiles) as he gave to us when we believed in the Lord Jesus Christ, who was I that I could withstand God?" *Justification for the mission to the Gentiles*

This section on the spread of the Church across Palestine ends with the account of the death of James (the brother of John) at the hands of Herod (Use your Bible Dictionary to get this Herod located), together with other persecutions of Jewish Christians. The time was coming to move outward to the Gentiles, a task for which Paul became an apostle (one sent out). *Persecution in Palestine*

Death of James

C. Expansion into Asia Minor and Europe

From here on out it is the Apostle Paul who will be the key figure in the book of Acts. It is he and his mission to the Gentiles that will eventually bring our story to Rome. We will divide this section of Acts into three parts, each dealing with one of Paul's missionary journeys into Asia Minor and Europe. Be sure to keep a map on hand as you read!

1. PAUL'S FIRST MISSIONARY JOURNEY
   READ: ACTS 13:1-15:36

It is hard to say whether Paul considered his three journeys into Asia Minor and Europe as journeys in the true sense. He really lived in the territory for extended periods and doubtless saw the whole eastern Mediterranean world as both his home and his mission.

Paul's missionary journeys

Paul's first extended journey is told about in Acts, chapters 13-14. Here we learn of the strategy that Paul was to use many times in different cities. He spoke first to the Jews in the local synagogue, and only afterward turned to the Gentiles of the area.

Acts 13-14: First thrust into Asia Minor

Chapter 15 tells a fascinating story of what is usually called the 'Council of Jerusalem.' The issues debated there became of paramount importance nearly everywhere Paul went and occupy much of his letter-writing preserved in our New Testament.

Council of Jerusalem in A.D. 46 ☆

The issue was basic: was it necessary to practice the old Jewish law, including circumcision, before one could become a Christian? Peter, Paul, and Barnabas all spoke in favor of putting no further burden upon Gentile converts than that of accepting God's grace. They carried the day in the debate and a group was commissioned to go to Antioch with a letter informing Gentile Christians there of the decision. Though the issue appeared settled, it continually cropped up wherever Paul went.

Circumcision → obediance to All Jewish laws.

The issue: Is circumcision to be required of Gentile converts?

> **TRY THIS**
>
> The Council of Jerusalem dealt with crucial issues for the Christian Church's future. Simply stated, the issue was this:
>
> Is circumcision required of Gentile converts?
>
> In reality the issue went much deeper than it appears. Circumcision obligated one to keep the whole law. It became a question of the way one related to God: through keeping of the law or by accepting the gift of his grace.
>
> When you have re-read Acts 15, divide your group

47

into the two parties in the dispute:

Judaizers: Those who believe circumcision and the law are the means (or pre-requisites) by which we relate to God, and who wish to require it of Gentile converts.

Paulinists: Those who, following Paul, believe our relation to God is by accepting his grace, not by following a law.

Be sure to allow each group to discuss their role so they are confident they understand their position.

Let each group develop a list of reasons for their position and record them on a large piece of paper. When each group has its stance firmly in hand, debate (that is, politely discuss!) the issues:

- What minimum standards should be set as Christianity spreads?
- Why the curious list the Council finally agreed upon?
- Where do you see these same issues in your congregation today?

The Gospel of salvation by *grace alone* was to become the watchword of Paul's lifelong ministry to the Gentiles.

2. PAUL'S SECOND MAJOR JOURNEY

   READ: ACTS 15:36-18:23

This whole section is worth reading because it contains the heart of Paul's mission to the region.

Paul decided to revisit the cities of Asia Minor in which he had already started a number of congregations on the first journey. From there he was led by a vision (16:9ff) to Macedonia, the region of northeastern Greece that had been the homeland of Alexander the Great. (Note here the abrupt shift to "we" on the part of the narrator.)

Asia Minor re-visited

PHILIPPI had no synagogue, but Paul met there a group of Jewish women who were in the habit of meeting by the river for prayer. From that nucleus emerged one of Paul's strongest new congregations, the first one in Europe, and one to whom he later wrote an eloquent letter.

A new congregation at Philippi

From Philippi Paul travelled the Via Egnatia, the old Roman road leading toward Athens. In THESSALONICA, BEROEA, and ATHENS he preached the Good News. If you follow this second journey on your map, you will get an idea of the rigor required - hundreds of miles and all of it on foot.

And others at:
Thessalonica
Beroea
Athens

Paul's ministry in CORINTH, another new congregation with which he later corresponded, was a stormy one. Troubles with Jewish opposition resulted in charges before the Roman Governor that Paul was teaching people to worship contrary to the Jewish law. It was the 'judaizing' controversy again, the same issue that had come before the Council of Jerusalem. Everywhere the Gospel was preached opposition arose, but everywhere there were also new congregations springing to life.

A stormy relationship with the new church at Corinth

D. The Gospel in Rome

READ: ACTS 18:23-19:41
21:1 - 23:35
27:1 - 28:31

Paul's THIRD MISSIONARY JOURNEY covered much the same territory as the second. In Acts 18:23-19:41, we have the account of Paul's extended stay in EPHESUS. This town was the center of the worship of Diana (Artemis in Greek), one of the most widespread cults of the Roman world. The account of the riot which took place there against Paul and the Christian faith is a vivid reminder of the controversy that universally accompanied the spread of the Church.

After re-tracing much of the pathway of his second journey, Paul was in a hurry to get back to Jerusalem in time for the celebration of Pentecost. His arrival there quickly aroused opposition, and in the uproar that followed, Paul was arrested. Feelings were so high that the Roman authorities feared for Paul's safety. In the dead of night they spirited him off to Caesarea on the coast where Paul languished in the Roman prison for two years. Finally, a new governor of the province agreed to hear Paul's case and accepted his appeal to Caesar in Rome. Thus began the final journey Paul had hoped to make as a free man.

Return to Jerusalem

Paul arrested, imprisoned at Caesarea

Paul appeals to Rome

The story of the trip to Rome is told in chapters 27-28 of Acts. They are as full of adventure as any in the New Testament. This is another of the "we" sections of the book, possibly suggesting that Luke was a participant. Give special attention to the story of the shipwreck on Malta. Could any but an eyewitness have written such an account?

The perilous journey to the city of Rome

The book of Acts ends with Paul under house-arrest in the city of Rome. He was able to receive visitors and to continue preaching in Jesus' name. Luke says that he was there for two years, but mysteriously does not tell us what happened.

Paul under house arrest, continues to preach

Tradition has it that Paul died in the persecution of Emperor Nero that broke out after the great fire of Rome in the year A.D. 64. While there is no evidence to confirm this, the tradition is an old one. Paul had come to Rome and Christianity had done so as well. While Luke does not explain how the faith preceded Paul to the capital, the book of Acts is a clear witness that the Gospel had penetrated the empire's heart. The stage was set for the conflict between Rome and Christ which occupies so much of the later New Testament.

The Gospel has come the full distance - from Jerusalem to Rome

IV. ISSUES AND ANSWERS

The story ACTS tells is one you want to go over slowly and digest. In it the issues to which *all* the other New Testament books are written can be seen emerging. A little time spent absorbing the ferment of which Acts tells will later be rewarded in your understanding of the larger picture the New Testament presents - which after all is one of the prime objectives of our study!

Can you sense the questions that practically exploded out of the experience of these first Christian congregations?

> If Jesus was the Messiah, why is God's kingdom not here?
> Do we prepare for the long haul of living in the Roman culture?
> Or do we forget all that and prepare for Christ's return?
> By what standards shall we live?
> How is being Christian different from being Jewish?
> How is being Christian different from Hellenistic culture or religion?
> How should we react to persecution?
> Who decides things when Christians disagree?

What raised most of these issues was not a desire to understand theology in an abstract way, but the need to decide *how to live*. Even for Paul, perhaps the New Testament's most intellectual writer, the issues of what to believe were always interrelated with decisions about living.

Paul's letters - the earliest writing in our New Testament- are almost entirely his reactions to questions like those above. Nowhere does he take the time to sit down and spell out his Christian faith in a systematic way until very late in his life when he penned a letter to Christians in Rome (probably during a short respite on his last visit to Corinth) as an introduction for his anticipated visit. With that exception, all of Paul's theology emerged out of the need to answer questions of Christian living for his former congregations.

Many of Paul's answers to inquiries from his churches were sharply controversial. The time Paul spends in his letters defending his apostolic authority makes it clear that many who disagreed with him questioned his right to a final word. The need to settle the arguments that characterized many of the new congregations gradually spawned two additional questions:

>   How would *Jesus* have acted? What did *he* do or say?

These were questions in which the writings of Paul show a curious lack of interest! And if Paul had settled all the issues of Christian living definitively, they might well have never come up. But they did, and the result was our Gospels. While that is a story to which we shall return later, it is worth noting now that the existence of *four* Gospels, each with a unique point of view on these issues, is itself testimony to the troublesome nature of these questions in the early Church.

From this it is not hard to see how a final set of questions very quickly arose:

>   What is the Church, and what is its authority?
>   Who governs the Church's life?
>   Who decides controversies?

It is no accident that the latest literature in the New Testament strongly reflects these latter concerns. We shall return to the issues of Church structure and organization near the end of our study, but it is important to realize that these issues were already present in the first years of the Church's life, and that as soon as apostolic authority disappeared (with the death of the apostles), these questions jumped into the forefront of the Church's concern.

Lastly, it is highly instructive to remind ourselves that it was neither the issues of Church organization, nor an account of Jesus' life that *first* consumed the energies of either new congregations or Christian writers. *First came the issues of how to live!* Virtually all other New Testament concerns arise out of that priority.

> **TRY THIS**
>
> Before you tackle the letters of Paul in the next chapter, you might reflect a little on your own experience in the Church and your reasons for studying the New Testament.
>
> 1. On a blank sheet of paper jot down two or three life-issues that are raised for you by virtue of being Christian in the contemporary world.
>
> 2. Beneath each issue, note where you would most likely seek help:
>
>   - from your Pastor? An Elder? (Do either of these have any 'apostolic' quality for you? Might you question their wisdom or authority as people did Paul's? Does even this suggestion seem ludicrous today?)
>   - From your reading of the Gospels? (That is, would you be inclined to seek out what *Jesus* did or said on the issue at hand?)

> -From your congregation or denomination?
> (That is, would you seek the wisdom of the
> Christian community?)
> -Elsewhere? Your own resources?
>
> 3. As time permits, persons in the group may wish
>   to share an item from their list. This kind of
>   group reflection will simulate the experience
>   of the early Christians.
>
>   Can you begin to sense why Paul wrote back to
>   former congregations?
>
> 4. Save your list for future reference as you
>   study the New Testament. You might even
>   collect references for further study should
>   any of your issues crop up as we go along.

For Budding New Testament Scholars: Extra-Curricular Activities

What we have done so far in our New Testament study may have encouraged you to try your hand at some historical/critical sleuthing of the type done by Biblical scholars in piecing together the life situation of New Testament writings. The exercises on the next page pose questions that Biblical scholars have actually tried to answer. In each instance our actual evidence is slim and a measure of creative imagination is needed.

Care to try your hand?

HISTORICAL/CRITICAL EXERCISES:

1. In four sections of ACTS, the narrator does an abrupt switch into the first person plural. He uses "we" instead of "they." Here are the four sections:

   Acts 16:10-17   20:5-15
        21:1-18   27:1-28:16

   Read the four sections and then ask yourself:

   Does this imply Luke himself participated in these four episodes?
   Does the writing style in the four differ from other parts of the book?
   Do they sound like eyewitness accounts?

2. Read the account of Paul's speech in Athens found in Acts 17:16-34 Then ask yourself:

   Does the speech sound like it fits the rather heated circumstances that precede it?

We know that ancient historians often composed speeches and put
them in the mouths of famous men. In doing so, they tried
to be faithful to their spokesman. Could this speech
in Acts 17 be a careful composition of Luke's?
Does the style of the speech provide any clues?

3. Luke gives us three versions of the conversion of Saul (later Paul) to Christianity. Here are the three accounts:

    Acts 9:1-22   Acts 22:1-22   Acts 26:1-29

It is difficult to know where Luke got the three versions of the story. Read them carefully, taking note of differences.

How should we account for these differences?
Why would Luke have told us the story three times?

These exercises will probably not yield definitive answers for you any more than for the trained scholar simply because our evidence is too skimpy. They should, however, give you an idea of the way Luke has woven together diverse traditions into a coherent narrative.

CHAPTER 4

Letters to new Congregations

To Galatia
To Corinth
To Philemon
To Philippi
To Colossi

"All of Paul's writing was letter writing. His only occasion for writing at all, so far as we know, was to communicate with his churches."

—J.E. Knox

* *

IN THIS CHAPTER WE WILL LOOK AT....

I. Paul's letters to New Congregations
   A. Concern for a struggling new church
      - I, II Thessalonians
   B. Issues of Christian living - I, II, Corinthians
   C. Clarifying the Christian message -
      Galatians, Colossians
   D. A letter to loyal friends - Philippians

II. A "Pauline" letter for all the churches - Ephesians

I. PAUL'S LETTERS TO NEW CONGREGATIONS

It may surprise you to learn how informally the writing of the New Testament began. The earliest Christian document we possess (I Thessalonians) was a letter Paul wrote to his friends in Thessalonica expressing his concern for their welfare. He had recently received news that things were going well, prompting him to write the letter expressing his delight. It was as simple and human as that.

The story in the book of Acts vividly describes the drama and turmoil that accompanied the spread of Christianity outside Palestine. From Paul's own hand we have an account of the dangers and hardships he suffered in carrying the message to the Mediterranean world that would quickly dispel any notions of a Sunday School outing (II Corinthians 11:16-29). It was no accident, therefore, that the correspondence of Paul in our New Testament is filled with intense emotion, colorful language, and even heated argument. By placing these letters in their proper life-situations, it is possible even today to sense the human drama they reflect.

A. CONCERN FOR A STRUGGLING NEW CHURCH

I AND II THESSALONIANS

Paul had stayed in Thessalonica for only a few weeks when serious conflict with the Jews resulted in a public uproar. Paul was forced to flee the city, along with co-workers Timothy and Silas (called Silvanus in the Thessalonian letters), and go by night to the nearby town of Beroea. After a brief visit there, Paul travelled to Athens by sea, and then on to Corinth for an extended stay. While in Corinth his anxiety about the struggling congregation he had been forced to leave behind in Thessalonica stirred him to send Timothy back to that city for a first-hand report. Not knowing what had become of the small congregation was more than Paul could stand.

> *The account of Paul's visit to Thessalonica is told in Acts 17. A quick review of the story will help clarify the background of Paul's Thessalonian correspondence.*
>
> *After you have re-read Acts 17, quickly look at I Thessalonians 2:17-3:10. Here Paul recounts his anxiety and Timothy's visit to ascertain the situation in Thessalonica.*

As soon as Timothy returned to Corinth with the news that the Christians there had remained loyal to the faith, Paul penned the letter we call I Thessalonians.

It expresses his relief at the good news, his delight in the growth of the new congregation, and gives brief answers to questions with which the Thessalonians were struggling. Both it and the second letter (which followed shortly) were written in about A. D. 50-51.

I THESSALONIANS

The letter is simple and brief. It easily divides into two main sections:
- Expressions of personal concern and thanksgiving 1:1-3:13
- Practical instruction on matters of faith 5:1-5:28

In the section of practical instruction, Paul has two concerns. Both apparently grew out of Timothy's report:

1. In light of the casual morality of the Roman world, Paul reminds the Thessalonians of the need to live exemplary lives in accord with the will of God.

2. In response to the Thessalonian's concerns that Christian friends who had already died might not participate in the experience of Christ's return, Paul reassures them that the dead in Christ shall rise at his coming. Those still alive should remain vigilant as they wait.

II THESSALONIANS

From the mood and contents of the second letter, it is clear that Paul's first effort had been misunderstood. Paul had counseled vigilance as they awaited Christ's return, but the Thessalonians took that to mean the event was coming immediately. They became caught up in speculation about its arrival. Some had stopped work and were living off Christian friends as they waited. Like many today who get excited about the end of the world, the Thessalonican Christians were in danger of becoming fanatical idlers.

Though some scholars today wonder if Paul is the true author of this second letter, the probability is that he is and that letter number two followed the first one by a very short time. It contains ideas and language that sound strange to the modern reader (and untypical of Paul), but it vividly portrays the excitement and fervor of the growing Christian community.

Read: I and II THESSALONIANS

B. ISSUES OF CHRISTIAN LIVING

I & II CORINTHIANS

Corinth was a rough city and Paul's relationship with the Church there was stormy from the beginning. The two letters in our New Testament which bear the name of this city are probably only a portion of Paul's actual correspondence with them, but within these two we possess enough detail to catch a glimpse of the turmoil.

> *The story of Paul's two visits to Corinth is told in Acts 18:1-18 and 20:1-3. A quick review will be helpful once again.*

For new converts and new congregations the problems of living in the pagan culture were difficult. Should they eat meat offered to pagan idols (much meat of this sort was re-sold in the public markets)? Should they marry non-believers? In light of Christ's expected return, should they marry at all?

Part of the difficulty grew out of the fact that Corinth, like many of the other congregations Paul started, was made up of people from widely diverse backgrounds. They often shared the Greek tendency to individualism and were more inclined to debate than cooperate. From looking at both the accounts of Paul's visits to Corinth in the book of Acts and the Corinthian letters themselves, it is clear that Paul had a hard time keeping the contentious bunch in Corinth together. Soon after he left, they had broken up into rival factions.

Paul probably wrote our I Corinthians from Ephesus in about A.D. 55-56. It was not, however, his first letter to this congregation. In I Corinthians 5:9 he mentions an earlier letter that had been misunderstood. Some scholars believe we have a fragment of that letter embedded in II Corinthians 6:24-7:1. From clues like this it is possible to reconstruct a possible scenario for Paul's letters and visits to Corinth that runs something like this:

A Possible Reconstruction of Paul's Corinthian Visits and Letters

1. Paul writes a first letter (now lost) after his first visit, warning of association with immoral Christians (See I Corinthians 5:9).
2. The Corinthian Church replies in a letter of their own (now lost).
3. Our I Corinthians is Paul's answer.
4. The conflict is not resolved. Paul visits Corinth again and has a bad time (Note the vague, brief account of this visit in Acts 20:1-3).
5. Paul writes a rather severe letter, which is painful to send (see II Corinthians 2:4 and 7:8), and decides to visit Corinth a third time (see II Corinthians 13:1).
6. Paul is worried over the Corinthian reaction. While enroute to visit Corinth he receives good news about the Church there from Titus.
7. Paul writes a happy, reconciling letter (portions of our II Corinthians) after receiving the good report.

I CORINTHIANS

This is the longest and most practical of all the letters Paul wrote. Yet in dealing with these matters of Christian living, Paul also takes every opportunity to reflect on the theological issues involved. This simple outline will help you follow Paul's train of thought as you read:

I. Factionalism in the Corinthian Church   1:1-3:21
   Paul argues that faith in Christ is superior to wisdom and knowledge, so prized in the contentious Hellenistic world.
II. Problems of Christian living   5:1-11:1
   Paul deals with the issue of litigation among Christians, with problems of sex and marriage, with scruples about eating meat offered to idols, and with the freedom of Christians in Christ.
III. Confusion in worship and the Lord's Supper   11:2-14:40
   The role of women in leading worship, and the confusion caused by greediness at communion meals are dealt with in sharp language. Paul suggests that the diversity of gifts among God's people are an occasion for unity, not strife.
IV. The resurrection   15:1-58
   In dealing with the question of resurrection, Paul gives us the earliest account we now have of the resurrection of Jesus (15:3-8).
V. Collections for the needy; personal matters   16:1-24

READ: I CORINTHIANS

II CORINTHIANS

The first letter to the Corinthian Christians had been a failure. The factionalism and moral confusion of the Corinthian Church continued unabated. Paul's second visit settled nothing either. Titus, sent to Corinth to help resolve the situation, had not returned to Ephesus, and Paul, in his anxiety over the trouble his angry letter may have caused, determined to set out for a third visit. Crossing over into Macedonia, he met the returning Titus who brought news of developments in Corinth. Paul's relief and thanksgiving are evident in his final letter, our II Corinthians.

Before you actually read II Corinthians, a little paste and scissors work might help sort things out:

A Possible Reconstruction of II Corinthians

> *If our reconstruction of events on page 57 is correct, it can be seen that Paul wrote as many as four letters to Corinth, of which our two are the second and fourth. Still another possibility is that II Corinthians as we have it is a paste and scissors job containing several letters or fragments thereof.*
>
> *I. Read II Corinthians 6:11-7:4. Does it appear to you that 6:14-7:1 do not belong in this section? Leave those verses out and read again (that is read 6:11-13 and jump to 7:2-4). Does it read more smoothly? Could 6:14-7 be an insert from another of Paul's Corinthian letters mistakenly put here by a later editor? Many scholars believe it is a fragment from a letter that is earlier than our I Corinthians.*
>
> *2. Look at the end of chapter 9. Does this sound like the end of a letter? Now look at chapter 10. Is this the beginning of a new one?*

> *It could be that chapters 10-13 are the severe letter spoken of earlier. Chapters 1-9 could be the reconciling letter written after the good report of Titus.*
>
> *3. If this reconstruction of the developments at Corinth is correct, the letter probably should be read this way:*
>
> | | |
> |---|---|
> | *The early fragment* | *II Corinthians 6:14-7:1* |
> | *The angry letter* | *II Corinthians chs. 10-13* |
> | *The news from Titus and the Letter of reconciliation* | *II Corinthians 1:1-6:13 and 7:2-9:15* |

READ: "II" CORINTHIANS

C. Clarifying The Christian Message

GALATIANS, COLOSSIANS

With the Gospel spreading rapidly into the turbulent Mediterranean world, it was almost inevitable that confusion over the message itself would arise. What does it mean to be Christian - as the followers of Jesus had come to be called? How is it different than being Jewish? Or a believer in Greek philosophy? Theological confusion and difference of opinion erupted almost everywhere Paul had gone as Christians tried to gain a sense of identity over against the culture and religion around them. Much of Paul's correspondence with his former churches reflects the Apostle's passionate concern for the clarity and truth of the Christian message.

GALATIANS

The letter to the Galatians is unmistakably from the hand of Paul. Its tone and intensity, together with the fascinating glimpses it offers of Paul's life, give us one of our clearest pictures of the great Apostle to the Gentiles.

The occasion and purpose of the letter to Galatia are easily understood. Early in his stay at Ephesus (Acts 19), Paul received news that teachers from the Church in Jerusalem were declaring that Gentiles must become Jews before they could become Christians, and that this opinion was making startling inroads among converts in Galatia. Paul refers to them as the 'circumcision party." These Jewish Christians sincerely believed that circumcision, which implied the obligation to keep the *whole* Jewish law, was required of all who wished to become part of the Church. They had intimidated Christians while visiting Antioch (including Peter! See Galatians 2:11 ff.), and were apparently doing so in Galatia as well. Paul was angry and said so!

Biblical scholars have long debated the destination of the Galatian letter. Was it written to the churches of Iconium, Derbe and Lystra - all cities in the Roman province of Galatia? Or was it addressed to the ethnic group known as Galatians living farther north in Asia Minor? While this question cannot be answered here, it is safe to say that the contents and style of the letter suggest that Paul wrote it in the same period as the Corinthian correspondence, perhaps from Ephesus in about A.D. 54.

The purpose of the letter is straightforward:

   a. Paul defends his authority as an apostle - and hence of the Gospel he has preached.

   b. Paul spells out the nature and validity of Christian freedom. For neither Jew nor Gentile is salvation possible through the law. Faith alone brings us the gift.

Paul is angry as he writes. In this letter alone he omits friendly notes of thanksgiving in the salutation. His vigorous reaction to the Judaizers (the circumcision party) is a clear tipoff that Paul believes something fundamental to be at stake.

> This simple outline of the book will help you as you read:
>
> I.   Paul's defense of apostleship and Gospel   Chapters 1-2
> II. Salvation by faith alone   3-4
> III. Ethics: freedom and spirit   5-6

READ: GALATIANS

➡️ *Two sections of Galatians hold special interest for the light they shed on Paul and his ministry. Give special attention to:*

   Galatians 1:10-14   Paul's autobiographical notes
   Galatians 2:1-10   Is this perhaps an earlier account of the Jerusalem Council in the year A.D. 46? Compare it with Acts 15.

COLOSSIANS

The story in the book of Acts ends with Paul a prisoner in Rome. There, under house arrest, he received visitors, wrote letters, and spoke with people about the Gospel. Three of Paul's letters were written from prison, possibly all three during this last imprisonment:

Paul's prison letters
- Philippians
- Colossians
- Philemon

(Ephesians is also a prison letter, but was likely written by a follower of Paul rather than the Apostle himself - more on this later.)

Two of these prison letters were sent to Colossae - one to the congregation there and the other (Philemon) to an individual whose slave had run away. Both letters were probably written at the same time and may have been sent to Colossae by the same messenger (see Col. 4:7-9).

The church at Colossae had been started by Epaphras, a fellow-worker with Paul in Asia Minor. Though Paul had never visited the congregation there, we can understand his concern when Epaphras visited him in Rome with a report of trouble in that church. Just as Paul had earlier been anxious to define the Christian faith in relation to Judaism, here near the end of his life he carries the same anxiety with respect to the influence of the religions and culture of the Roman world which Epaphras reports are causing confusion.

If Paul wrote Colossians from Rome - and there is some evidence that the letter is neither from Rome nor genuinely Pauline - it would have been sent in about A. D. 61. Paul writes to warn and encourage a church which is in danger of being overwhelmed by false teaching. Exactly what this false teaching was, we do not know, but its broad outlines can be deduced from the contents of Paul's letter.

Paul seems to be addressing two major issues in Colossians:

a. In contrast to pagan influence promoting the worship of angels or cosmic beings as intermediaries between us and God, Paul declares that Christ alone was the one in whom "all the fulness of God was pleased to dwell."

b. Against those who were turning Christianity into a secret knowledge reserved for the initiated elite, Paul argues once again that salvation is God's gift to all through faith.

The Colossian heresy would have turned Christianity into a class system and denied the supremacy of Christ. Both issues were to plague the Church for many centuries, but here, near the end of his life, Paul displays once again his unerring sense of the fundamental nature of the faith.

> This simple outline will again aid your reading:
>
> | | | |
> |---|---|---|
> | I. | Greetings to friends | Chapter 1:1-14 |
> | II. | The supremacy of Christ | 1:15-2:7 |
> | III. | Salvation by faith alone | 2:8-23 |
> | IV. | Issues of Christian conduct | 3:1-4:6 |
> | V. | Farewell salutations | 4:7-18 |

READ: COLOSSIANS

A note on the letter to Philemon

> We will not be looking at this little book in detail, but for all its brevity, it represents a dramatic note in church life. Onesimus, a runaway slave, came to Paul in Rome seeking help. In Roman society runaways were punished by death. Paul sends Onesimus back to Colossae with a letter urging Philemon, his Christian master, to treat him with compassion and forbearance.

D. A Letter to Loyal Friends

PHILIPPIANS

PHILIPPIANS is the other letter Paul wrote from prison in Rome. In keeping with our overview style, we cannot deal with every letter in detail, yet we must not pass over the Philippian letter as if it were unimportant. It is the most intimate and happy of all the letters Paul wrote for former friends.

Paul was apparently unwilling to accept financial aid from any congregation except that in Philippi. The occasion for this letter was an unsolicited gift from the Philippian Christians which Paul wished to acknowledge. He gives thanks for friends who have supported him in good times and bad. Although the letter acknowledges the peril Paul now realizes is engulfing him, the tone of the letter is warm and encouraging.

If you take the time to read Philippians now, you may also want to refresh your memory about Paul's ministry there. The story is told in Acts 16.

II. A "Pauline" Letter for All the Churches

EPHESIANS

Up until the ninteenth century of our era it was assumed that the letter we call 'Ephesians' was written by Paul from prison in Rome. The letter itself suggests that. Since that time, however, most Biblical scholars have come to agreement that the letter was written by a devoted follower of Paul, not by Paul himself. It might have been written as a 'cover letter' to the collection of Paul's letters that began to circulate through the Church near the end of the first century.

The problems in the book are many. First, there is the question of the letter's intended recipients. The phrase "in Ephesus" (1:1) we now know was not in the original letter. It was added by a Scribe in the fourth century. This immediately makes the letter a general communication rather than a specific one to a particular church.

The problem of authorship is difficult too. Its style is not typical of Paul. Not only is it written for a general audience (unlike any other known Pauline letter), but also its language, contents, and style are quite different from letters we are confident Paul wrote.

Other problems appear as well. The writer seems unacquainted with his audience (see 1:5 and 3:1), and yet Paul had labored in Ephesus for nearly three years. Even when Paul's typical language or style are used, they appear in quite original and different ways. Lastly, there is the fact that the letter implies a highly developed church life that is at variance with Paul's earlier attitudes. To many, this argues for a date later in the first century.

At first it may seem upsetting that a book purportedly written by Paul may not have been. We know, however, that it was common in the early Church to write in a great Apostle's name as an honest and sincere attempt to develop apostolic thought in new and creative ways. Many scholars now believe that a devoted and faithful follower of Paul, who may have known the Apostle personally, penned Ephesians as a cover letter at the time the whole corpus of Paul's correspondence was collected for circulation across the Church.

We conclude, then, that Ephesians is the work of a first century follower of Paul who brought to life again Paul's concern for the unity and purity of the Church. In flowing and eloquent language the writer declares the strife and discord of society will be overcome in the unity of the body of Christ.

Ephesians does not break down into a simple outline. In addition to its greetings and farewell, it shows two major themes:

    I. The unity of all things in Christ   Chapters 1-3
    II. Ethical encouragement and instructions   4-6

READ: EPHESIANS

TRY THIS

Paul's letters come out of the actual experience of the first Christian congregations. They are specific and practical - meant to be of help to Christians struggling with their faith in difficult circumstances.

1. On a large sheet of paper, have your group brainstorm a list of problems to which letters such as Paul's might be addressed in our day. Keep the specifics of your own experience and congregation in mind.

    You might do it this way:

PROBLEMS OF LIVING	PROBLEMS OF THEOLOGY
1. Population explosion	1. Interpreting the N.T.
2. Racism	2. Renewing worship
3. Care of the aged	3. Understanding God
4. etc.	4. etc.

2. If possible, pick out one of your practical problems of Christian living and discuss within the group potential confusions of belief that could result from the various ways Christians today are handling the ethical issue.

3. Now try the same thing in reverse. Pick one of your areas of theological confusion and discuss what problems are raised thereby for making decisions about how to live.

Belief and practice are always intertwined in Paul's letters. In what ways does your discussion show that to be true today?

The letters of Paul, together with the book we call Ephesians, constitute nearly one-fourth of the New Testament. They are the earliest Christian writings we still possess, and surely among the most valuable. The issues and problems to which they are addressed are still alive today, though in admittedly transposed form. Paul's clarification of the essential nature of faith in Christ forms the foundation for us as Christians now, as well as the backdrop against which we shall soon begin to understand the Gospels.

Before turning to the Gospel's accounts of Jesus' life, however, we must give special attention to Paul's letter to the Romans. We have saved it until last, not because it was written last, but because it represents the most comprehensive and profound summary of Paul's faith that we possess. It deserves a brief, though special, chapter all its own.

CHAPTER 5

To Rome... The Gospel according to Paul...

the gospel according to
PAUL

Romans represents Paul's clearest and most inclusive statement of the Gospel as he knew it. It is our boldest manifesto of the faith.

* *

IN THIS CHAPTER WE WILL LOOK AT....

I. Romans: Paul's Exposition of the Gospel
    A. The circumstances of writing: An anticipated visit
    B. The key question: How is sinful humanity to be accounted righteous before God?
    C. The thread of Paul's argument

II. The Heart of Paul's Faith

I. Romans: Paul's Exposition of the Gospel

Throughout our discussion of the letters of Paul, we have emphasized the way each letter was addressed to specific needs in particular churches. Each was the result of problems that had occurred in Paul's ministry with a congregation, and most of the letters reflect the intense emotion and turmoil of the growing Church.

Romans is an exception to this pattern. It is the only one of Paul's letters in which he had the time for a carefully thought out explanation of the Gospel as he knew it. It is thus one of the longest and most profound of all Paul's writings. It is the kind of book that has repaid a lifetime of study to many who have seen in it a theological depth and sensitivity unlike any outside the Gospels. Romans is Paul's considered statement of his own faith.

A. The Circumstances of Writing: An Anticipated Visit

Eager to make the Gospel known throughout the Mediterranean world, Paul had concentrated first on its eastern half. With strong congregations now scattered throughout this eastern region, each in turn spawning new outreaches of its own, Paul was free to turn his attention to the west, and especially to the capital city of Rome.

One thing stood in his way. In his travels through Macedonia and Greece on what we have called his third missionary journey, Paul had been taking a collection for the poverty-stricken Christians of Jerusalem. With delegates from the Gentile churches, Paul planned to visit Jerusalem and deliver the aid in person. While waiting in Corinth for that journey to Jerusalem to commence, Paul took advantage of the time to sit down and write to the Christians in Rome of his intention to visit them when the matter in Jerusalem was completed. We can thus date Romans at about A.D. 56-57.

Christianity had preceded Paul to Rome, though Acts does not tell us exactly how it arrived. From hard experience Paul had learned of the struggles new congregations went through as they sought to distinguish the Gospel from Judaism on the one hand, and the religions of the Empire on the other. He also knew of the controversy his own message might engender among Christians who had never met him and had already learned of the Gospel from other sources. In order to introduce himself and to prepare the Roman Church for his visit, Paul determined to lay out his understanding of the Gospel for them as completely as he could. The result was our New Testament book of Romans.

B. The Key Question: How is Sinful Humanity to be Accounted Righteous Before God?

Paul's hard experience among his new congregations of the eastern Empire had given him a keen sense of the fundamental issues. Among Jewish Christians there was the tendency to turn Christianity into a new legalism, as if Christ had come to bring a new and deeper kind of law. Such would have made salvation a matter of renewed effort at obedience, and Christ a moral task master. Among

Hellenistic Christians there was the tendency to turn Christianity into a new philosophy or system of divine knowledge. This would have made salvation a matter of education in the divine mysteries, and Christ would have become merely another philosophical ideal.

Paul saw that neither Jewish legalism nor Hellenistic divine knowledge addressed the desperate human situation adequately. For Paul, the answer was faith in the righteousness and grace of God.

The Greeks had said, "To know the good is to do the good," They saw the human problem as a lack of knowledge about how to live, and were confident that once initiated in true knowledge, good lives would naturally follow. Paul saw that the human problem is far deeper: we know the good and have no power to do it. We often do evil in spite of knowing what is right.

The Jews had said, "Follow God's law." They saw our difficulty as a matter of inadequate resolve in measuring up to the law God has given. To them renewed moral effort was the answer. Yet Paul saw that this left us exactly where we were with the Greeks: with *knowledge* of what God wants and *no power* in ourselves to pull it off.

Paul sensed that the question of acceptability before God (which is after all only an extension of the question about our sense of worth to ourselves) has introduced a certain desperation into the human situation. The quest can drive one mad. Each law brings only the possibility of a new one yet unfulfilled. Each bit of knowledge brings only the awareness of what more one does not know. There is always just beyond the horizon the threat that what I have done is not enough. There is always more. How much goodness or how much knowledge does it take to make me worthy?

For Paul the only answer is to abandon the quest altogether. No person, by moral striving or dedicated effort, can ever match the law's demands. The only answer to the question of how sinful humanity can be accounted righteous before God is to accept by faith the acceptability God gives us as a gift. There is nothing to earn. There is only the gift to receive.

This gift changed Paul's life. Like Augustine, Luther, Calvin and countless other Christians after him, Paul had found a new freedom, a new exhilaration in living, and a new sense of his own worth once he abandoned the quest for acceptability and relied upon the grace of God. The profound nature of this transformation makes it easier for us to understand why Paul was such a vehement opponent of both Judaizers and those who would turn Christianity into another Hellenistic religion. Both would have made faith into a renewed quest, and made the death and resurrection of Christ of no value. Clarity on this issue was fundamental to the future of the Gospel.

It is to this issue that the book of Romans is addressed. Before coming to Rome, and especially in light of his fear that false teachers may have preceded him to the capital, Paul wished to make his case for salvation by faith in God's unmerited gift. The whole book of Romans centers on this theme. The mood often varies, the pace changes, other phases of the subject are explored, but the theme is always the same. Romans 1:16-17 states it succinctly:

"For I am not ashamed of the Gospel. It is the saving power of God for everyone who has faith - the Jew first, but the Greek also - because here is revealed God's way of righting wrong, a way that starts in faith and ends in faith; as Scripture says, 'He shall gain life who is justified through faith'."

C. The Thread of Paul's Argument

The book of Romans is more like a theological argument than any other New Testament book, and is best understood when it can be seen in its entirety. Each new point Paul makes is built upon a previous argument, hence we need to gain an overview of the whole to understand the parts.

> **THE THEME OF ROMANS**
>
> Paul has already introduced the theme of the book in the first part of Chapter One:
>
> Acceptability before God is a gift. It is unearned and unearnable. It is accepted by trusting God's graciousness, that is, by faith.

(1) THE HUMAN CONDITION   ROMANS 1:18-3:20

Paul gives an extensive account of the human condition. He concludes that sin has pervaded the entire human race, both Jew and Gentile alike.

Gentiles, Paul argues, might have known God by observing creation. Instead they replaced the Creator with the creature and worshipped themselves.   *1:18-2:16*

The Jews who might have been expected to be better off since they had the advantage of the law, are alienated from God as well. The law though known, has not been kept. Jews and Greeks (here a synonym for all Gentiles) alike are under the power of sin.   *2:17-3:20*

(2) JUSTIFIED BY GOD'S GRACE

The answer to the human problem is neither law nor knowledge, but faith. God's grace, freely given, declares us righteous when we are not. By the sacrificial death of Jesus, both Jew and Gentile are justified before God.   *3:21-31*

(3) ABRAHAM: FAITH'S EXAMPLE

For Jews, who might have looked to their tradition as proof of the essential, central and irrevocable place of the law in our relationship to God, Paul cites their ancestor Abraham as the pioneer and example of justification by faith.   *4:1-25*

(4) GOD'S GRACE AND HUMAN FREEDOM

Because of God's love to us in Christ, the
Christian lives a new life in this old world,
even while salvation is incomplete and the world   5:1-21
continues to decay. Because of Christ the
whole situation has begun to change.

The curse of the law was that even though it
gave us knowledge of what God requires, it could
not break the hold evil has over our lives.   6:1-23
But for the person of faith, the power of sin
is broken.

Nor is the person who accepts God's grace by
faith any longer under the burden of a law he
cannot fulfill. We are freed from the law, not   7:1-25
because moral conduct does not matter, but because
it is a futile means of winning God's favor.

Freed from the power of sin and death, the person
of faith is filled with the Spirit of life. This
new life in God's Spirit convinces Paul that nothing 8:1-39
in all the world can separate us from the love of God.

(5) GOD'S ULTIMATE FAITHFULNESS TO JEWS

On Paul's own terms, the nation of Israel does
not seem to be inheriting the ancient promise.
Yet Paul argues that in spite of Israel's
faithlessness to God, God will at length melt   Chapters 9-11
Jewish hearts and all Israel will return to him.

(6) THE LIFE OF FAITH

As in all of Paul's letters, theology is never
separated from life. Hence Paul spells out
concrete examples of the way the new freedom of
faith works in the life of the Christian. For
Paul, freedom from the law leads not to anarchy   Chapters 12-15
and lawlessness, but to the life of love.

➤ *Chapter 16 of Romans has long been a puzzle to
Biblical scholars. It consists of a greeting to
"our sister Phoebe" and a long series of salutations to no less than twenty-four persons by name.
How could Paul have known so many persons in a
city he had never visited?*

*Another curious fact is that most of the names in
Chapter 16 are Greek rather than Roman, and many*

> *were associated with Paul in his work at*
> *Ephesus! For this and other reasons, many*
> *scholars believe the last chapter to be a*
> *separate note intended for the Church in*
> *Ephesus. How it came to be attached to the letter*
> *to Rome we do not know, though it could have*
> *happened at the time the Pauline letters were*
> *collected and circulated.*

With this survey of Paul's argument in the letter to Rome still fresh in your mind, now is the time to read the book. It may help you to read the letter section by section, first reviewing our summary of the argument and then reading the appropriate section of Romans.

READ: ROMANS

II The Heart of Paul's Faith

It should be evident by now that the book of Romans declares the heart of Paul's faith. It is his clearest and most profound statement of the Gospel as he knew it. It is without a doubt one of the high points of the New Testament, and that is our justification for dealing with the book in as much detail as we have. Paul's whole life and career are to be understood in light of this summary statement of his Gospel.

One of the curious characteristics of Romans, and of all of Paul's other writings as well, is their lack of interest in the details of Jesus' life. Even Paul's account of the resurrection of Jesus in I Corinthians 15 (the earliest such account we possess) is no more than the barest statement of the facts:

> First and foremost, I handed on to you the facts which had been
> imparted to me: that Christ died for our sins, in accordance with
> the Scriptures; that he was buried; that he was raised to life on
> the third day, according to the Scriptures; and that he appeared to
> Cephas, and afterward to the Twelve. Then he appeared to over
> five hundred of our brothers at once, most of whom are still alive,
> though some have died. Then he appeared to James, and afterwards
> to all the apostles.

This represents as full an account of Jesus' life as Paul ever gives. Many have wondered, Why?

In our next chapter we shall see the peculiar situations in the life of the early Church that finally led to an intense interest in the details of Jesus' earthly life. Though many reasons have been suggested to explain why Paul had no such interest, perhaps the most important is simply that Paul was concerned with the *meaning* of Jesus, rather than mere facts about him, because it was the meaning of Jesus that addressed those crucial issues of our relation to God with which the first century world was engrossed. Paul's own Jewish theological heritage, together with his encounter with the religious tumult of the Greco-Roman world, placed him at the heart of the emerging Church's struggle to understand itself and its message. It was thus the theological meaning of Jesus and the lifestyle of the Christian that absorbed the interest and energy of the great Apostle to the Gentiles.

In that same fifteenth chapter of I Corinthians, Paul concludes his brief account of Jesus' resurrection by adding:

"Last of all, as to one untimely born, he appeared also to me."

The experience on the road to Damascus (Acts 9) had been decisive. The persecutor became the persecuted. The one who was unfit to become an apostle became the greatest of them all, not by his own doing, but by the mysterious grace of God.

It was thus the graciousness of God that for Paul became the heart of his faith. All his letters in one way or another are only variations on that theme. 'In Christ' everything has become new. Neither Judaizers on the one hand, nor Hellenistic philosophies on the other, could divert Paul's attention from the fundamental experience of faith in God's grace.

> **TRY THIS**
>
> Though the concept of faith as trust in God is not difficult to understand, the ways in which we replace faith with subtle schemes for trusting ourselves are quite another matter. Since most such schemes parade under the guise of positively good efforts, it is difficult to see them as the enemy of faith.
>
> A good example is the way we sometimes substitute the performance of religious practices for faith in God. We assume that if...
>   You attend church regularly
>   You pray frequently
>   You give of your time and money
>
> God will surely like you. How could he do otherwise? Can you see that all these things, good as they are, can become a standard by which we judge whether or not God would count us worthy?
>
> The point of 'faith' is that there are *no* such standards. God's love is unearned and unearnable. It is purely a gift.
>
> 1. Most of us confront the question of our 'acceptability' in relation to each other and ourselves more readily than we do in relation to God.
>
>   Give each person a magazine or two (any magazine

with an abundance of pictures) and ask them to tear out a few pictures or words that express our human struggle for acceptability to ourselves and each other.

2. Lay the torn-out pieces on the floor (or on the table if the group is seated around one) in the center of the group so that everyone can see the collection. Using specific words or pictures in front of you for illustration, let the group discuss for a few minutes the following question:

> How pervasive is the struggle for acceptability in our lives?

Perhaps this exercise will suggest to you how fundamental to all of life the problem of achieving acceptability is. Paul believed that at the root of this horizontal, human struggle was the issue of our acceptability before God, and that no human scheme, however good, provided an answer. All schemes merely complicate the quagmire. Faith - abandoning the quest - is to accept God's gift of life and know there is nothing to prove or attain.

CHAPTER 6

The Synoptic Gospels:
PORTRAITS OF JESUS

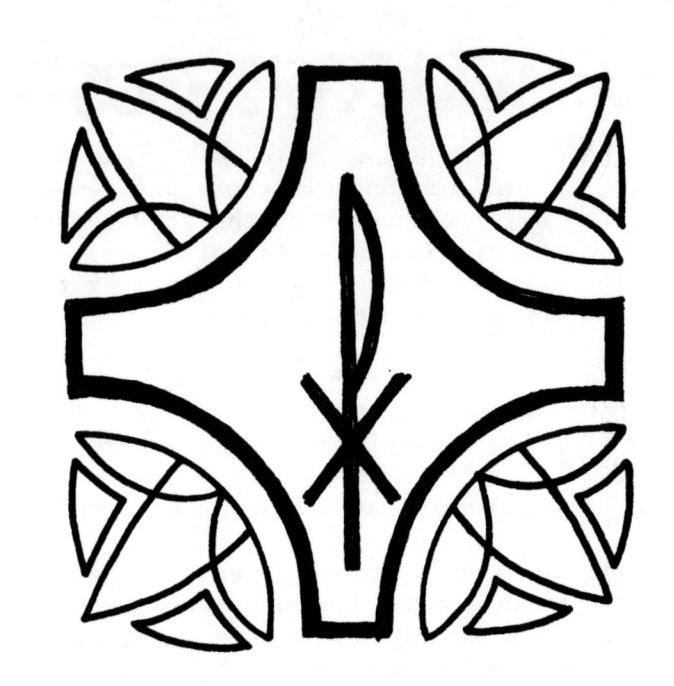

"Imagine a Syrian Orthodox scribe, an Italian civil service employee, a British man of letters, and a Franciscan monk writing simultaneously on a common subject of mutually immense significance, and you have approximated the differences that characterize the four Gospels."

— W. G. Rollins

* *

IN THIS CHAPTER WE WILL LOOK AT....

    I.   The written Gospel
        A.   From 'Christ-event' to written Gospel
        B.   The Gospel and the Gospels

    II. Studying the Gospels
        A.   The synoptic problem
        B.   Tools and methods for synoptic study

I. THE WRITTEN GOSPEL

In the popular mind the Gospels represent simple biographical stories about Jesus written by eyewitnesses to the actual events. They are also among the best-known parts of the New Testament. Many of the sayings of Jesus as well as the major events of his life are familiar to people both in and outside the contemporary Christian community.

The actual character and significance of our written Gospels is much richer and more complex than is usually supposed. They are not really biographies in the usual sense - they show little interest in the personal details or history of Jesus' life - nor are they simple collections of stories. Each is a sensitive, *theological interpretation* of Jesus shaped by the vision of the writer and the needs of the Church. Hence it will richly enhance our 'overview' objective if we take the time to see how the Gospels came into being and how they met the needs of the Church. Some new methods, which are especially valuable in the study of the Gospels, must also be added to our bag of tools. Our purpose will be to see how the oral Gospel, taught by Paul and other early preachers, eventually became the written Gospels in our New Testament.

A. FROM CHRIST-EVENT TO WRITTEN GOSPEL

In telling the story of the letters of Paul, we acknowledged that everything began with the events of Jesus' life, death and resurrection.* Scholars refer to this core of the Christian story as the "Christ-event". The term encompasses all of those original events of Jesus' life which can now be experienced only through the eyes of second-hand witnesses. Much that we do not know, but would dearly like to know, is lost forever in the unrecorded memories of those who had known Jesus in their lifetimes. Unavailable as much of this is, however, it is this *unwritten* story of the historical Jesus that is the foundation upon which the written Gospels stand.

In a culture in which only a privileged few could read and write, it was natural that the first reports of the Christ-event would be oral. People shared by word-of-mouth what they remembered Jesus having said and done. In excitement, enthusiasm, disbelief, or even anger, people spread the news. "Did you hear him say...?" "You should have seen what he did today..." Out of just such shared memories developed a body of circulating material we now call the *oral tradition*. It represented the first step in the spread of the Good News.

People today are inclined to be sceptical about the value of anything passed along by word-of-mouth. We know the penchant people have for getting the message garbled. In ancient times, however, the preservation of oral tradition was taken with great seriousness simply because it had to be. It was the only means of saving material and handing it down among people who could not read and write. This is not to say that the sayings of Jesus were not remembered

---

The story of the growth of the New Testament writings, including the Gospels, was outlined in Chapter 2. You may want to review that material before going further.

differently in different parts of the Church, or that they were not shaped by
the creative uses to which they were put, but rather that we should not judge
the oral tradition by modern practices. It had an important role to play in
ancient society and in the spread of the Gospel.

A crucial part of the oral tradition was the preaching of the early evangelists.
In their sermons (for example, those of Peter and Paul recorded in Acts) we
see glimpses of the way the tradition about Jesus was used in the life of the
Church. Much of this preaching shows a surprising lack of interest in the
details of Jesus' life. Instead, we find a passionate proclamation of
the whole Christ-event with a strong appeal for faith and acceptance.
The familiar Gospel stories of Jesus play only an incidental role.

Yet inevitably these evangelists would have used the sayings of Jesus, anecdotes
from his life, and accounts of his death and resurrection as illustrations in
their preaching. In the course of instructing further those who responded to
the appeal, other parts of the story of Jesus would have been recalled and
eventually written down. These small units of the story (or pericopes as
scholars call them) may first have been collected orally and then gradually
reduced to writing to meet the needs of the Church.

Various collections of this material would have served special needs. Parables
and sayings of Jesus would have been useful in teaching new converts, or in
preaching during worship services. Prayers of Jesus would also have been an
aid to worship. Since the significance of Jesus' death formed a major part
of the apostolic message, the story of the crucifixion would naturally have been
a key aid in teaching and preaching, and hence was probably among the first
portions of the story written down. Crucifixion stories may also have been a
help in explaining to critics why Jesus was crucified even though avowedly
guiltless. Moreover, to those facing persecution and possible martyrdom, it may
have been an inspiration and encouragement to know how Jesus faced death.

As we shall see in more detail later, these and other factors help explain why
the Church preserved and eventually wrote down certain traditions about Jesus
while others were quickly lost from memory. Thus Matthew, a Gospel apparently
written for teaching and instruction in the Church, preserves sayings and
teachings of Jesus that the other Gospel writers either did not know or felt
were of secondary importance. Likewise, Luke tells stories that are unique to
his Gospel (the Good Samaritan, the Prodigal Son, etc.), and presumably of special
value to Luke's particular audience.

It is important to see that the memory of the Church and the Gospel writers was
selective, and that by this very selectivity each of the Gospel writers has
given the tradition handed down to him a unique shape and color. None of our
Gospels is mere news reporting. Each is a highly interpretive selection of the
tradition, shaped to meet the needs of particular churches, and written to
express the unique faith of the author. Each writer worked with a collection of
both oral and written material before him, arranging it and shaping it to
speak to a particular group of people. Each was what we call a *redactor*,
that is, an *editor* of tradition who sought to give coherence to the story. Each
Gospel author is thus a theologian in his own right whose particular view of
Jesus can greatly enrich the Church.

Much of the oral tradition, of course, is lost to us forever. The same is true
of much of the written tradition about Jesus. A number of Gospels were written

in the early Church which have not survived to our day. Others have recently
come to light again such as the well-known gnostic writing we call the GOSPEL
ACCORDING TO THOMAS. It was unearthed in an Egyptian village in 1945. While
few of these non-canonical Gospels provide reliable information for our study of
Jesus, they do shed fascinating light on the scope and variety of the tradition
that circulated in the early Church. It is no wonder that persons such as
Luke were concerned for the accuracy of what was being handed on:

> "Inasmuch as many have undertaken to compile a narrative of
> things which have been accomplished among us, just as they were
> delivered to us by those who from the beginning were eyewitnesses
> and ministers of the word, so it seemed good to me also, having
> followed all these things closely for some time past, to write
> an orderly account for you, most excellent Theophilus, that
> you may know the truth concerning the things of which you have
> been informed."
>
> Luke 1:1-4

Each of the Gospels, then, must be studied in its own right, because each
sees Jesus in the unique light. Each writer is an artist fashioning an expression
of his own faith in Jesus out of the traditions handed down to him. Each has taken
the received tradition, both written and oral, and given it the stamp of his own
personality and thought. Each wrote in different circumstances, to a different
audience, with widely variant needs of the Church in mind. Even though each of
the Gospels is the story of Jesus, each is at the same time a confession of faith
on the part of its author.

B. The Gospel and The Gospels

The word 'Gospel' is simply Old English for 'good news'. Its original meaning
referred not to a book, but to an oral proclamation. The same is true of the
original Greek term for Gospel, *euangelion*, from which we get our word evangelism.
To the New Testament writers this term stood for the announcement that in
Jesus, God had acted decisively to save us from sin and death. Mark 1:15 reports
Jesus coming into Galilee preaching:

> "The time is fulfilled, the kingdom of God is at hand, repent and
> believe the Gospel."

For Mark, that is a summary of the whole Christ-event. But not only for Mark,
because each of the New Testament writers would doubtless have characterized
the Gospel in very nearly that way. The term 'Gospel' thus stands for the *whole*
of what God has done in the life, death and resurrection of Jesus.

Nowadays, however, we are used to making a plural out of the word when we refer
to the four 'Gospels'. To avoid confusion, it is worth noting the titles to
these four books as they are printed in our New Testament. They are called:
"*The* Gospel *According to* Matthew," "*The* Gospel *According to* Mark," and so on.
That is, each is a variant on a single theme - *the* Gospel. It is the *one* Gospel
as seen through the eyes of Matthew or Mark that we are reading, not a different
Gospel given to us by each author. While it is true that each author gives the
story in unique coloring, and that the study of this uniqueness is a rewarding
one, at the same time it is important to remember that it is the *one thing* that
God has done in Jesus that is *the* Gospel to which each writer bears his own
witness.

II. Studying the Gospels

Detailed study of the Gospels has proven to be a gold mine of easily overlooked riches. It is sometimes hard for modern readers to appreciate the depth of what is involved, so familiar are we with the surface meanings of well-known Gospel passages. Often the deceptive simplicity of the language catches our ear and prevents a deeper look. Yet with a few tools and background understandings, the study of the Gospels can become one of the great treasures of the New Testament.

In this section of our study we shall be looking only at Matthew, Mark and Luke. These three Gospels are called by scholars the *Synoptics*. The term 'synoptic' means to *see together;* that is, these three Gospels present a remarkably similar view of Jesus and his ministry and can easily be studied side by side. It is obvious to even the casual reader that the Gospel According to John is so different than the other three that it must be studied in a different context. We shall get to this Johannine literature later in our study, but for now, our concern will be the Synoptic Gospels.

A. The Synoptic Problem

One of the basic problems of New Testament study is the attempt to discover the relationship of the Gospels to each other. Matthew, Mark and Luke are so similar in vocabulary, content and sequence of events, that viewing them together makes what differences they do exhibit all the more striking and worthy of study. This kind of *comparative* look at the three Synoptics is a fascinating and rewarding enterprise.

The so-called 'synoptic problem' is the result of trying to explain both the similarities and the differences in the three synoptic Gospels. It was once widely believed that all three synoptic authors had a common oral or written source, thus accounting for their similarity. Careful study, however, has since made it obvious that Mark was the first Gospel written and was itself a major source for the writing of the other two.

When passages from the three synoptics are set side by side in parallel columns for easier study, several striking facts emerge. In both sequence of events and in the wordings of particular passages, all three are frequently identical. When the three do diverge, however, a pattern is evident that makes clear Mark's priority. For example, when Matthew and Luke are using non-Markan material, they do not agree on where to place it in Mark's sequence of events. Matthew places the Sermon on the Mount at one point in the story, but Luke has it at a very different place. Or again, when Matthew and Luke are using Mark's work they often have variant readings in which Matthew may agree with Mark while Luke differs, or Luke may agree with Mark while Matthew differs, but Matthew and Luke do not agree with each other against Mark.

It is obvious, therefore, that Mark is the common factor and that both Matthew and Luke must have had Mark in front of them when they wrote. While we cannot take time here to spell out the many complex factors that support this conclusion, we can say that virtually all New Testament scholars agree that Mark was written first and that both Matthew and Luke used Mark as one of their sources.

Perhaps this diagram will help make the relationship among the Synoptics clearer. When Matthew and Luke are using Mark's material:

| MARK | *...and MATTHEW often agree while LUKE differs* |
| MARK | *...and LUKE often agree while MATTHEW differs* |

BUT....

MATTHEW and LUKE almost never agree against MARK

HENCE...

MARK   *is the common factor*

Before we try to put the whole synoptic picture together (and pause for examples of comparative study), we need several more parts of the puzzle. Both Matthew and Luke seem to know a common source that Mark did not use. This collection of sayings of Jesus is usually called "Q" by scholars (from the German word *Quelle*, meaning 'source'). In addition, Matthew and Luke each have material that is uniquely theirs. We can label this uniquely Matthean material "M", and the material that is in Luke alone "L". We thus end up with a jigsaw puzzle that looks something like this:

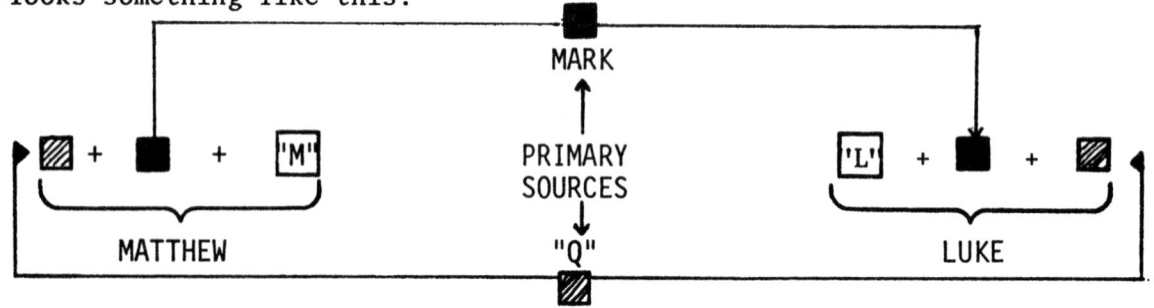

```
                            MARK
                             ↑
   ▨ + ■ + 'M'         PRIMARY         'L' + ■ + ▨
   ⎵⎵⎵⎵⎵⎵⎵            SOURCES         ⎵⎵⎵⎵⎵⎵⎵
    MATTHEW              "Q"              LUKE
                          ↓
                          ▨
```

Look closely at the diagram. It shows that Mark is a primary source. So also is "Q". Matthew is thus a composite of material from Mark, additional material from "Q", and Matthew's own special material we have called "M". Luke is a similar composit. It consists of Mark, Q, and Luke's own tradition, L. If this hypothesis is correct, and it is widely accepted by New Testament scholars, we will be able to learn some fascinating and important things about the life and ministry of Jesus by comparing the way each of the synoptic writers has handled this complex tradition. In order to do that, we need a couple of simple tools.

B. Tools and Methods for Synoptic Study

Of the 661 verses in our English versions of the Gospel according to Mark, 600 of them are in Matthew. 350 of these same verses are in Luke. It will be well worth our time to take note of the way the three writers handle this material they share in common. In order to do this kind of synoptic study easily, you may want to obtain what is called a *Gospel Parallels*. A good one available in most bookstores is:

> GOSPEL PARALLELS
> Thomas Nelson and Sons
> New York, 1957

The GOSPEL PARALLELS prints the three synoptic Gospels in parallel columns for quick, handy reference. Here is an example:

Mark 15:39	Matthew 27:54	Luke 23-47
And when the centurion, who stood facing him, saw that he thus breathed his last, he said, "**Truly this man was a son of God!**"	When the centurion and those who were with him, keeping watch over Jesus, saw the earthquake and what took place, they were filled with awe, and said, "**Truly this was a son of God!**"	Now when the centurion saw what had taken place, he praised God, and said, "**Certainly this man was innocent!**"

It is obvious that with the material printed out in parallel columns like this the differences and similarities among the three Gospels are more graphic. A *Gospel Parallels* is inexpensive and you may want to purchase one for further study.

Since we have the above example from the passion stories in front of us, we should take the time to ask about the differences in these accounts as an illustration of what can be learned by this kind of comparative study. You will see that while Matthew gives slightly more detail than Mark, these two versions are substantially the same. Especially important is the fact that the quotation is virtually the same in both Gospels.

Luke's account, however, is significantly different. The quotation of the Roman centurion is not at all like that in Matthew and Mark. What can we make of this? Did the centurion say both things? That is possible. But it is also possible that Luke has transposed the tradition for the understanding of his special audience. Luke was a Gentile, writing to Gentiles, who knew little of the messianic significance of the term "son of God." For Gentile audiences the key difficulty might have been that of believing in a Savior who had been judged guilty by Roman law. Luke had to show his readers that Jesus was not just another malefactor who received his due reward from the Roman authorities. In Luke's mind, Jesus was an *innocent* victim - not that the other Gospel writers would have disagreed, but for Luke this was a particularly important item to make clear for his audience. So who is it in the story that declares Jesus innocent? The Roman centurion!

Some modern readers will be perplexed by the kind of problems this comparative study of the Gospels presents. They will want to know what 'really happened.' Unfortunately we do not know what really happened in many instances, and probably never will know, because the Gospel writers did not deem it of great significance to tell us. They wanted us to know the *meaning* of what was going on, and that they tell us with great insight. Jesus *was* the suffering son of God to Matthew and Mark, and he *was* the innocent victim of human cruelty to Luke - both things are true about Jesus - and each author has used his arrangement of the events in the story as a vehicle to show us that particular meaning about Jesus he wants us to see.

Another fascinating and rich aspect of Synoptic study is a comparative look at Matthew and Luke's treatment of Q - the hypothetical source of Jesus' sayings they share in common. Much of Q is teaching material, and the two authors treat it very differently. In Matthew many of these sayings have been collected into large blocks of teaching that seem to come from Jesus' lips at one time and place. An example of this is the so-called Sermon on the Mount (Matthew 5-7). In Luke, however, this same material is less systematically collected, often set in different contexts and geographical locales, and sometimes worded differently. Ponder this example:

Matthew 5:3	Luke 6:20
"Blessed are the **poor in spirit**, for theirs is the kingdom of heaven."	"Blessed are you **poor**, for yours is the kingdom of God."

Why has Matthew spiritualized the saying? Or is it Luke that has materialized it? While we do not know which form is the original, or even if Jesus said it both ways, it is important to see the form in which each writer remembered the saying and what Jesus meant to him in light of it.

Lastly, any comparative study of the Synoptics must draw attention to the nature of M and L - the material unique to Matthew and Luke. We do not know where these writers got this tradition, but we can safely assume that it had particular meaning for them or they would not have included it. Here is a partial list of the contents of M and L:

"M"	Matthew
Coming of the wise men	2:1-12
Jesus' words on the law	5:17-20
Comfort for the heavy-laden	11:28-30
Parable of the weeds	13:24-30
Parable of the ten virgins	25:1-13

"L"	Luke
Story of the shepherds	2:1-20
Jesus at twelve years	2:41-52
Parable of the Prodigal	15:11-32
Parable of the Good Samaritan	10:29-37
Emmaus Road story	24:13-27

Once again our question will be, Why? Why did Matthew and Luke find these stories important? How did they come to know them? Why did other writers not know them? Or did they, and did they not deem them worth recording? While definitive answers to these questions are often not available to us now, studying these and similar questions will frequently offer us a way to unlock riches in the Gospels that the casual reader overlooks.

C. OUR OBJECTIVES IN STUDYING THE SYNOPTICS

In summary, then, we are going to do a bit of sleuthing in each of the Synoptics to see if we can uncover some of these treasures the casual reader often misses. Our purpose will be to gain a small bit of insight into the way the Gospels might have been read by those for whom they were first written, so that we will have enriched the base from which to ask about their meaning for our own lives today.

In keeping with our overview objective, we will look for the major thrust of each author's message. While space will not permit a detailed look at many individual passages in the Synoptics, the reader should find that his later study of these smaller units will have gained clarity and depth as a result of seeing the larger picture.

We shall be looking for the structure or outline of each book as well, thus clarifying the writer's basic intention. We shall note particular emphases of each Gospel, together with important peculiarities in the way each author has handled the tradition. Out of this should come a sense of the way each Gospel author has shaped what he received in order to meet the needs of his particular audience. While all of this is a big order in a few pages, and cannot be done in great detail, it should lead us to some sense of perspective for reading the Gospels in our own time.

WE WILL BE:

1. *Setting each Gospel in its proper historical context*
2. *Relating the material to the life of the early Church*
3. *Uncovering the major emphases and structure of each Gospel*
4. *Making synoptic comparisons*
5. *Observing material unique to a single Gospel (The "M" and "L" material)*

6. *Comparing Matthew's and Luke's use of "Q"*
7. *Summarizing each Gospel's major thrust*

Finally, we shall invite the reader to ask about the meaning of the Gospel in our own day - which is, after all, the point of our study in the first place. It is the meaning of Jesus *now* which gives us reason to study the meaning of Jesus *then*.

TRY THIS

A little time spent in reminiscing might help you get a feel for the selectivity of the memory of the Church in relation to Jesus. There are a lot of ways to do this; here are a few suggestions:

1. Go around your group and ask people to share briefly their memory of significant events like:

    The bombing of Pearl Harbor
    The assassination of John F. Kennedy
    V-J Day
    Neil Armstrong's moon landing

    People often remember *where they were* when these things happened. Why is this?

2. Another way to think about selective memory is to share childhood experiences. Let the group share childhood memories that are particularly important to them such as: one's first day in public school, or a significant birthday, or any other event remembered as having high significance. Ask yourselves:

    Why this particular memory?
    What is its meaning now?
    Have my feelings about it changed with time?

3. A third way of sharing memories might be to find a recent event shared by all or most of the group:

    A television program
    A movie
    A recent worship service or sermon
    A public event

    Then let all who witnessed the event share their memory of it and what was significant about it.

Any of these exercises should produce widely varied memories and perceptions about the past. The key questions in all of the discussion should be:

Why this particular memory or perception?
How is each individual's memory related to his/her particular needs or way of viewing things?

After such a discussion it will perhaps be easier to understand the significance of the term 'selective memory' when applied to the Gospels, and why the comparative study of them is so rewarding.

CHAPTER 7

JESUS XHRIST IS LORD

THE GOSPEL ACCORDING TO MARK

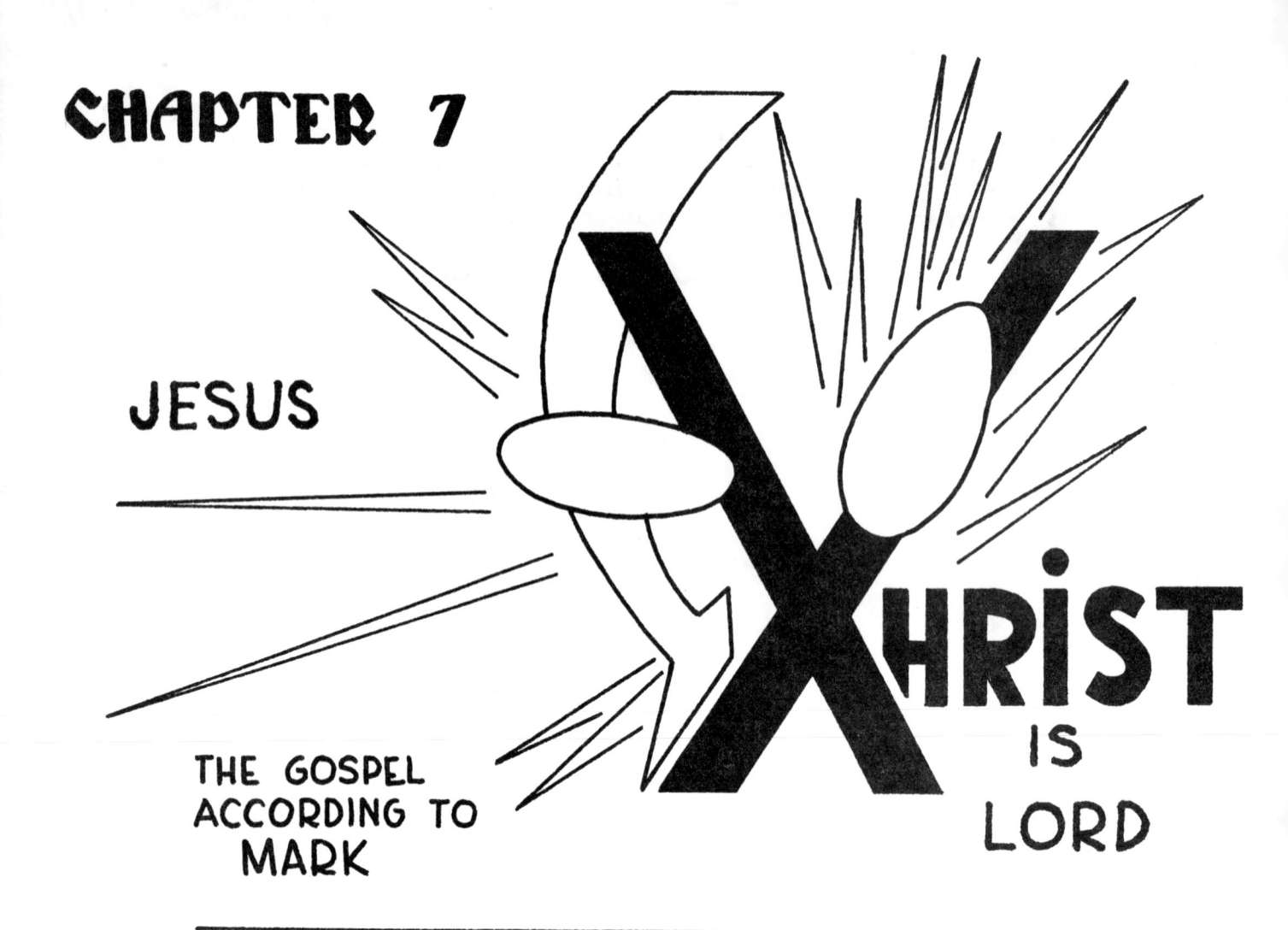

Early Christians asked, 'If Jesus brought God's kingdom, why are we facing death?' Mark's answer: it is in suffering and death that God has confounded and defeated the powers of the world. That is the Good News!

* *

IN THIS CHAPTER WE WILL LOOK AT.....
- I. The Gospel According to Mark
    - A. The structure of Mark
    - B. Conflict and Good News
    - C. The Messiah and the coming Passion
    - D. The Passion narrative
    - E. Epilogue: the future victory

- II. The Gospel, According to Mark

I. The Gospel According to Mark

From what evidence we have available, it appears likely that Mark was the first Gospel written. Tradition has attributed its authorship to the John Mark who was a companion of Paul and a close associate of Peter. Though the Gospel itself names no author, and though all four Gospels were probably read as anonymous works by the first Christian readers, still this Gospel's association with the name of Mark is very old. So also is the tradition that Mark is essentially a spokesman for Peter.

About the year A.D. 140, Papias, a Bishop of the early Church, bore testimony to the Gospel's origin:

> This also the elder used to say: "Mark, indeed, who became the interpreter of Peter, wrote accurately, as far as he remembered the things done or said by the Lord, but not however in order. For he (Mark) had neither heard the Lord nor been his personal follower, but at a later stage, as I said, he had followed Peter, who used to adapt the teachings to the needs of the moment, but not as though he were drawing up a connected account of the oracles of the Lord; so that Mark committed no error in writing certain matters just as he remembered them. For he had only one object in view, namely to leave out nothing of the things he had heard, and to include no false statement among them."

Though full of fascinating hints, the statement is not without problems that leave room for much scholarly disagreement. Nonetheless, most New Testament scholars accept the general tradition that Mark was a spokesman for Peter.

From what we have said so far, it should not be difficult to sense the importance of this tradition associating Mark with Peter. Eyewitnesses were dying off, confusion and misunderstanding were growing, persecutions threatened, and it quickly became of critical importance that the Church preserve the witness of those who had been with Jesus personally. Peter, surely one of Jesus' more colorful interpreters, probably died in the persecutions of Nero near A.D. 64, yet if the ancient tradition is correct, his legacy was not lost but is preserved for us in the composition of this first Gospel.

The date of Mark's Gospel is usually inferred from the text itself. Mark 13:2 seems to imply that the temple of Jerusalem was still standing. 13:14 suggests that the destruction of the temple is either imminent or has just happened. Since this great event did occur in A.D. 70, it is possible to date Mark immediately before or after that year.

Early tradition also testifies that the Gospel was written in Rome for a Gentile Christian audience. Both the text of the Gospel and the events of the period tend to corroborate this tradition. At several points (5:41; 7:3, 11, 34; 15:22) Mark assumes that his readers are ignorant of Jewish practices - hence we infer they were Gentiles. Mark's emphasis on persecution (which we shall see in more detail later) admirably fits the events of the mid-sixties in and around Rome. The famed fire of Rome during which Nero fiddled (which may or may not be true), together with the persecution of Christians which followed, gave ample justification for a story of Jesus which stressed his suffering, death and triumph. To Christians faced with the prospect of dying for their faith, the recollections of Peter (who according to the tradition was crucified, head downward) about the meaning of Jesus' suffering would have been a rich treasure to write down and preserve.

A. The Structure of Mark

To the casual reader the Gospel According to Mark may appear a loosely connected series of anecdotes about Jesus. The comment of Papias that Mark got his material from Peter in somewhat random fashion seems to be confirmed by the breathless stringing together of events that Mark gives us. The whole Gospel gives the impression of a rapid-fire, candid portrait written with a great sense of urgency.

For example, look at Mark's opening. There is no thoughtful prologue as in John, nor any birth stories as in Matthew and Luke, just this crashing opening:

"The beginning of the Gospel of Jesus Christ, the Son of God."

In the fifteen short verses that follow, Jesus is baptized by John, who has come into the wilderness to announce the coming of God's kingdom, the Spirit of God descends and a voice declares, 'You are my Son, the Beloved; my favor rests upon you,' Jesus is driven into the wilderness and tempted by Satan, John is arrested, and Jesus comes into the region of Galilee preaching:

"The time is fulfilled, the kingdom of God is at hand; repent and believe in the Gospel!"

With that the ministry of Jesus is launched - 'immediately,' to use a favorite term of Mark's. Good news has erupted in our midst!

Here is a simple outline of Mark that will help you get the picture:	
I. Prologue: Announcing the Kingdom	1:1-1:13
II. Conflict and Good News	1:13-8:26
III. The Messiah and the Coming Passion	8:27-10:52
IV. The Passion Narrative	11:1 - 14:47
V. Epilogue: The Future Victory	16:1-8

You will note that 16:9-20 have been left out of the above outline. Since none of the earliest manuscripts includes these verses, the probability is that they were not a part of the original Gospel. Was the ending lost? No one knows. Vss. 9-20 could be from Mark's hand, or from that of a later Scribe who felt the work was unfinished. As the earliest texts have it, however, the work ends with 16:8.

Before we leave the question of the Gospel's structure, we must comment upon its major parts. Leaving aside the prologue and epilogue for a moment, the Gospel easily breaks down into two major sections with a pivotal series of episodes between them. The first major section is a loosely connected series of stories about Jesus' ministry in and around the region of Galilee. Here Jesus is in constant conflict with demons, disease, Pharisees and temple authorities. Out of these conflicts emerges the key question Mark's Gospel addresses: Who is Jesus and by what power does he do these things?

Most interpreters regard the event at Caesarea Philippi (8:27-9:1) as the key to understanding the whole Gospel. Here the recurring issue of Jesus' identity is bluntly put before the disciples by Jesus himself:

"Who do men say that I am?"

From this and the following episodes of this central section of the Gospel, it is clear that neither the populace nor the disciples really understood. It would not be until Jesus faced death and emerged triumphant that his true identity would be fully grasped.

The final major section of the Gospel is the extended passion narrative. With some justification this Gospel has been called a "passion story with an extended introduction," because it is in the climax of Jesus' death and resurrection that Mark finds the Good News concealed. For Mark, it is in conflict, suffering and death that God has come to announce the long-awaited kingdom. It is in resurrection that suffering and death will be turned into triumph for both Jesus and those who follow.

B. Conflict and Good News

With the major thrust of Mark in front of us, let us take a closer look at passages in each of the three major sections we have summarized. This will give us not only the opportunity for a deeper look at Mark, but a chance to use some of our new tools for the study of the Synoptics.

The first major section of Mark tells the story of conflict. Jesus casts out demons, heals disease, debates with the Pharisees and causes much uproar. Throughout this section Mark stresses the power of Jesus and the confusion about his identity that is caused by it. A struggle is going on - one that begins immediately after Jesus' baptism in the conflict between the Spirit and Satan as Jesus is tempted (1:12-13). Soon it moves to a new level, that of Jesus and the powers of evil loose in the world. As we shall see shortly, the conflict deepens as Jesus confronts the Pharisees and the misunderstandings of his own disciples, and will end only as Jesus (like the early Christians) faces the ultimate enemy, death.

At each level of the conflict, the identity of Jesus is confused. Miracles and exhibitions of power curiously do not produce disciples. In the end it will be failure - death - that finally reveals both the true identity of Jesus and the true power of God.

Look at the story of Jesus casting out a demon while in the Synagogue of Capernaum (Mark 1:21-28). Opposition between the teaching of Jesus and that of the Scribes colors the background. Jesus teaches with an astonishing sense of authority, and yet no one in the crowd seems to recognize Jesus except the demon. He cries out, "I know who you are, the Holy One of God." Only the demon recognizes that Jesus has come to destroy the power of evil. Violence, shouting and crying out occur. After Jesus has cast out the demon there is amazement, silence, and the spread of Jesus' fame.

But there are no new disciples. The display of power causes astonishment but little else. After many of the conflicts of this opening section of Mark in which Jesus effects some display of power, he goes so far as to command silence about him from those involved. This so-called 'messianic secret' is one of the curious features of Mark's account (See also 1:43ff.; 3:12; 5:43). It is clear that in displays of power few will properly understand Jesus' mission and identity. His power thus must be kept quiet until its true dimensions can be seen.

While we are dealing with this story in Mark it might also be good to make use of synoptic comparisons. If you read this story in Luke (4:31-37), you will see that Luke has it substantially the same as it appears in Mark. Luke's dependence on Mark is obvious. In Matthew, however, both the situation and the story are quite different.

Matthew does not tell the story of the exorcism, he only records the opening statement about Jesus not teaching as the Scribes do (7:28-29). Moreover, the statement is not set within the context of an incident in the Synagogue of Capernaum. In Matthew, it is the conclusion of a long discourse of Jesus we now call the Sermon on the Mount. To Matthew the statement about Jesus teaching with authority fits appropriately as the conclusion of just such a long collection of Jesus' teaching.

Since Matthew had Mark in front of him when he wrote, it appears as if he has deliberately detached the statement about Jesus from its Markan setting and used it for his own purposes in another context. As we shall see in the next chapter, it is Jesus' teaching that interests Matthew - hence his use of the statement. For Mark, however, it is the action of Jesus in the midst of conflict that is of primary concern, because it is in that arena that Jesus' identity will eventually emerge. Each writer has thus used this statement about Jesus in a way that suits his overall purpose.

TRY THIS

The identity of Jesus is an issue of perennial confusion in the Church today just as it was in Mark's time. We shall be back to this central concern many times in our course of study, but for now, your group might try the following as a way to begin looking at the issue:

1. Allow any persons who will to share with the group stories from their own experience (or that they have heard from a friend) about the 'power' of Jesus. It may be an incident of unusual guidance or aid, or some particularly eventful 'answer to prayer.'

   To some people these stories are very real, while to

> others they are quite incredible. Such as they are, let a few in the group share episodes they have heard about or experienced.
>
> 2. From the background elicited above, brainstorm on a blackboard what these stories imply about the meaning or identity of Jesus. Ask yourselves questions like:
>
>   - In what ways, if any, are these episodes a key to understanding Jesus?
>   - What do they imply about the power of God?
>   - Why do some people believe them while others call them fantasy?
>   - Do they clarify Jesus' role in our lives, or do they muddy the water?
>
> 3. Perhaps you will find yourselves disagreeing over the answers to these questions. If so, you will have approximated the effect the healings and other displays of power by Jesus produced among his hearers.
>
> 4. Now ask yourselves this one:
>
>   Jesus (or was it Mark?) wanted such displays of power hushed up for fear of confusion over his true identity and mission. In light of this, what use should we make of these stories in Mark today?

C. The Messiah and the Coming Passion

The opposition to Jesus came not only from demonic forces, but also from the religious establishment. The stories of Jesus' debates with the Pharisees (which we have not taken time to consider in detail) suggest that these debates were matters of life and death. From that time on the opposition began to plot Jesus' destruction.

According to Mark, Jesus also knew that death would be the outcome of the struggle. Three times in the Gospel Jesus predicts his own death (8:32; 9:32; 10:35). Each of the death-predictions is followed by a response from the disciples showing they did not understand or accept what Jesus told them. Jesus reaffirms the prediction by applying it to the disciples and showing that they must anticipate the same kind of suffering. The message to the suffering Christians of the year A.D. 70 is unmistakably clear.

The key to this section, and indeed to the entire Gospel of Mark, is the episode recounted in 8:27-33. There the question of Jesus' identity is bluntly put, and for the first time - here in the context of a prediction of death - the disciples identify Jesus as the Messiah (Greek: *Christos*). Strangely, as the drama intensifies and the question of identity is brought out into the open, Jesus again tells his followers to keep his messiahship secret. The disciples may have labeled Jesus, but they have not yet understood. Even in the following episode (usually called the 'transfiguration') in which Jesus is revealed as the kingly Son of God (9:2-13), the disciples are told to keep quiet about him. The time for full understanding has not yet come.

Sandwiched between these two important episodes - Peter's confession of Jesus as the Messiah and the transfiguration - is the call to take up the cross and follow. What is coming for the Master will come for the disciple as well. In Jesus' suffering will the ultimate meaning of the suffering of his followers be revealed. Mark (Jesus) is calling the beleaguered Gentile Christians around Rome to follow even unto death.

D. The Passion Narrative

After the drama and conflict of Jesus' actions throughout the Gospel, the story of Jesus' death strikes a different kind of mood. Jesus is passive. He takes no action. He cannot avoid the suffering, and quietly hears his claim to save others mocked by those who shout that he cannot save himself. It is not in the exercise of power, but in his obedience unto death that Jesus saves others, an irony that Mark has chosen to highlight.

Earlier we suggested that the passion narratives may have been one of those pericopes that circulated independently before the composition of our Gospels. The story is remarkably similar in all three Synoptics, though each author gives the story his own emphasis. Before we go further, we suggest taking time out to read Mark's passion story in its entirety.

READ: MARK 14:1-15:47

Many commentators have pointed to Jesus' cry of dereliction (15:34) as the key to Mark's passion story. Jesus cries out:

> "My God, my God, why have you forsaken me?"

Is it a cry of despair? Or one of victory? The cry is a quotation from Psalm 22 which begins with this same cry and yet ends with a song of triumph. Perhaps the cry merely presages the final victory.

Yet even if the cry implies the final triumph, here in the context of defeat and gloom Mark surely wishes the suffering Christians of his time to see that the fear of abandonment, the confusion and despair that they themselves were undergoing, had been experienced before them in the ultimate degree by Jesus himself. And at the same time, since the cry is a prayer addressed to God, it implies that neither Jesus nor the disciples in their hour of defeat will finally be abandoned.

It is fitting that in the end a Roman centurion is the one to confess Jesus as God's son. At Jesus' baptism and at the transfiguration, this designation of

Jesus had been announced by a voice from heaven. Now it is confessed by one like those for whom the Gospel is intended, a Gentile. Moreover, the meaning of the term - which displays of power led people to misunderstand - is finally clarified in death: Jesus, by his suffering (and by the suffering of all who follow the Master) brings God's kingdom into being.

E. Epilogue: The Future Victory

We all know that the story ends in resurrection. But in Mark, more than in any of the other Gospels, the note of triumph is restrained. There is the bare announcement of the empty tomb and the frightened reaction of the women, but nothing more. We have already noted that the original text of Mark ended with verse 8 so that the Gospel ends with an expression of fear not unlike that which must have gripped the early Church. Final victory remained in the future and demanded faith. In faith, the disciple is called to follow Jesus.

II. The Gospel, According to Mark

The major thrust of Mark's Good News is clear: Jesus has brought in the kingdom of God by his suffering and death, not by displays of power. In following him, all who suffer with him will understand his meaning as God's Son. It is only *after* death (and resurrection) that the disciples know who Jesus really is.

On reflection, the Gospel According to Mark is not the simple and uncomplicated composition it appears to be on the surface. Leaving aside much detail and explanation, Mark weaves a story of confusion, conflict and misunderstanding which eventually leads to Jesus' death. In the first half of the Gospel the arena is Jesus' struggle with Pharisees, disease, and demons. From the watershed chapter 8 onward, the focus is increasingly the disciples and their confused efforts to understand. By selecting material with this emphasis Mark indicates his understanding of the feelings of the Church - the first century disciples who did not understand. If Jesus had brought victory and the kingdom, why were they facing death? Mark's answer: it is in suffering and death that God has confounded and defeated the powers of evil. *That* is the Good News!

> *Now is the time to read the Gospel According to Mark. You will gain the most from your reading if you use a translation with which you are **not** familiar - preferably a modern one. This will lend a small measure of freshness to your reading which, if possible, should be done at one sitting.*

TRY THIS

For Mark, the meaning of Jesus is seen in suffering, not in displays of power. For us today, the temptation to interpret Jesus' meaning in our lives in terms of power is still very real. But suppose we were to try to look at Jesus through Mark's eyes. Where would we look to hear Jesus' voice today?

1. Collect current magazines and newspapers that describe current events. Divide your group into two parts as follows:

    a. Let one group make a collage depicting displays of power or success. This could include headlines about natural events, or political episodes, or personal dramas.

    b. Let this group make a similar collage depicting the human suffering of our world. Both pictures and headlines could be used. Try to picture suffering the victims could not avoid as opposed to that produced by their own mistakes.

2. Place both collages in the center of your group on the floor or table. Then discuss the possibilities for understanding Jesus in light of each. You may discover something of him in both collages, but in either case, ask yourselves in what ways the struggle in which Jesus died is still going on. Finally, try the tough one:

    Is suffering still redemptive today?

OR

TRY THIS

As an alternative for attempting to understand the struggle of Jesus in contemporary terms, you might arrange a showing of the movie COOL HAND LUKE. The story is loosely based on the life of Jesus and you should be able to identify many of the incidents from Mark's Gospel in the film. Your group could then discuss:

- In what ways is Luke a 'Christ' figure?
- Is his suffering redemptive?
- Is the film's version of redemption like that of the Gospel?
- In what ways is redemption the outcome of suffering today?

CHAPTER 8

THE GOSPEL ACCORDING TO MATTHEW

A CALL TO RADICAL OBEDIENCE

In the Gospel as Matthew describes it, Christianity is not an accident or a new beginning, it is a promised consummation.

* *

IN THIS CHAPTER WE WILL LOOK AT.....

I. The Gospel According to Matthew
    A. The setting, the audience, the author, the style.
    B. Jesus (Matthew) as teacher
    C. The coming kingdom: a drama in seven acts

II. The Gospel, according to Matthew

I. The Gospel According to Matthew

Within a few decades of its writing, the Gospel According to Matthew was quoted by Ignatius (Bishop of Antioch, A.D. 110-115) as "the Gospel". By the end of the second century, it had achieved a position of first rank in the life of the Church, and Christian writers were quoting it more frequently than any other New Testament document. Not because it was written first, but because it stood first in usefulness to the Church, this Gospel According to Matthew was placed first in the canon and has maintained that rank ever since.

A. The Setting

Picture the Roman world in the year A.D. 90: civil wars, provincial uprisings, incredible brutality, overwhelming poverty existing alongside fabulous wealth, exploitation and oppression of non-Romans, almost total moral breakdown coming side by side with new religious cults popping up all over the landscape. Fire, thunder, whirlwinds and an earthquake or two seemed to be coming from all sides at once. It was a turbulent and fearsome age.

It was especially so for a Christian. Severe persecutions had periodically broken out, and one clearly risked his neck if he was too public about being a follower of Jesus. People had that terrible, indefinable feeling that something momentous was going to happen. It had to; things could just not go on like they were.

Relations between Christians and Jews were becoming increasingly difficult as well. After the destruction of Jerusalem and the Temple in A.D. 70, Judaism began to retrench. Threatened extinction led to the development of a Pharisaic uniformity that would not tolerate sectarian movements such as Jewish Christianity. To both Jew and Jewish Christian, the destruction of the Temple raised questions about the future of God's dealings with his people. Who would be the heir of the promise? The resulting tension between Pharisee and Christian is in plain view in the Gospel According to Matthew (See ch. 23).

THE AUDIENCE

Matthew, more than any of our other Gospels, is written to and for the Church. The Gospel is cast in the form of a manual for instruction and may well have been written especially for new Christians (catechumens) wondering what in the world they were getting into. You can imagine the questions and fears they might have had:

- Who is this Jesus they call the Messiah?
- What might it cost me to follow him?
- What was he like? What did he say? Why did he so affect people?

- How are we to survive the coming fire-storm? Will God help us?
- How is a Christian supposed to act in these times?
- What about our leaders - aren't they taking terrible risks in public?

Since many of Matthew's readers were probably Jewish Christians, they might have had several of their own questions to ponder:

- Is this what it is all coming to? Is God's old promise to his people all going to end in nothing?
- What about our old heritage - will it be lost? Forgotten?

Given all that the Good News promised, still, it was a difficult time in which to accept the faith and be baptized. A hundred questions flooding the hearts of new Christians might in the end have come down to this one:

- How are we to be rescued from this evil age? Who will save us?

Matthew's answer is that Jesus, the Expected One, Emmanuel (God is with us), is our Savior and King. Sit at his feet like a disciple and you will learn...

THE AUTHOR

We do not know who wrote the Gospel to which Matthew's name is attached. Papias (Do you recall his comment about Mark?) gives us what may be the earliest reference to the Gospel (A.D. 140):

> "Matthew compiled the reports in the Hebrew language and each interpreted them as best he could."

Our Gospel, however, was written in Greek. Papias could be referring to a Matthean tradition (Q???) that lay behind our Gospel, or he and others in the early Christian community may have *assumed* Matthean authorship from the following:

Matthew 9:9	Mark 2:14
"As Jesus passed on from there he saw a man called **Matthew** sitting there at the tax office; and he said to him, 'Follow me!'"	"And as he passed on, he saw **Levi**, son of Alphaeus, sitting at the tax office; and he said to him, 'Follow me!'"

(You might also compare Matthew 10:3 and Mark 3:18)

Whoever wrote the book - he is unnamed in the text - he was likely a Jewish Christian writing to Greek-speaking Christians. Many of his readers may have been Jewish Christians themselves. Our author may even have been a Jewish Scribe. Note this one:

Matthew 26:47	Mark 14:13
"...Judas came, one of the twelve, and with him a crowd with swords and clubs, from the chief priests and the elders of the people."	"...Judas came, one of the twelve, and with him a crowd with swords and clubs, from the chief priests **and the scribes** and the elders."

On several such occasions 'Matthew' cuts the scribes out of the black-hat role. Could that be because he was one himself?

THE DATE

Such sleuthing around in the text of Matthew itself may also provide a clue to the date of the Gospel's composition. Read very carefully Matthew's account of the parable of the marriage feast. It is found in 22:1-14. Now compare it with the account in Luke 14:16-24 (Here is a good occasion for using your *Gospel Parallels* if you bought one!). What do you make of Matthew's addition of the words:

> "The king was angry, and he sent his troops and destroyed those murderers and burned their city."

Is this a reference to the destruction of Jerusalem in A.D. 70? Even more, is it a commentary of Matthew (Jesus?) on the then current disarray of the Jewish community?

The implication seems to be that Matthew was written *after* the fall of the Temple. Since Matthew uses Mark so extensively, it would also had to have been written after Mark had gained some prominence. A good guess would be A.D. 80-100, probably in Syria (the location of its earliest use).

THE STYLE

Eleven times in the Gospel According to Matthew we read, "...thus was fulfilled what was spoken by the prophet..." More than any other New Testament book, Matthew stresses the Old Testament being fulfilled in the New. This was the traditional *pesher* method (*pesher* is Hebrew for, 'this refers to such and such ...') of the rabbis by which they sought new meanings in old references. It was a teaching method, and indeed, Matthew is above all a *teaching* Gospel.

Many scholars have suggested that Matthew might have been a manual for teaching catechumens (new Christians studying for baptism). If that is so, then we have here the early Church's judgement about what a new Christian should know about Jesus. Matthew's concern was that his fellow Christians see Jesus as the fulfillment of the Old Testament heritage, not a rejection of it. That can be clearly seen in the following synoptic comparison (The talk about old wine and new wine is here symbolic of the old covenant and the new one which has come in Jesus):

Mark 2:22	Luke 5:39	Matthew 9:17
"...but new wine is for fresh skins."	"...and no one after drinking old wine desires new; for he says, 'The old is good!'"	"...but new wine is put into new skins, and **so both are preserved**."

We do not know what Jesus actually said, we simply observe Mark wanting to get on with the new, Luke anxious to stress the ancient heritage of the faith to his Gentile readers who might have viewed Christianity as just another fly-by-night religion, and Matthew eager to tell his Jewish audience that the new does not negate the old, but rather both will be preserved.

B. Jesus (Matthew) as Teacher

Matthew's Gospel is the teaching Gospel par excellence. Not only does it contain more of Jesus' teaching than any other New Testament source, but also it is neat, orderly and well thought out. Jesus is, of course, the true teacher, but the way Matthew has collected, codified, edited and arranged his sources makes it clear that Matthew too has a message. He, not only Jesus, becomes the teacher of the community.

Matthew has collected the sayings and teachings of Jesus into five sections or 'books'. In doing so, it seems probable that Matthew has attempted to mimic the five books of Moses (The Torah: Genesis, Exodus, Leviticus, Numbers and Deuteronomy). Moses, of course, was the great lawgiver and teacher of Israel. Jesus is the teacher of the new Israel, the Church, and so, for Matthew, the sayings of Jesus are the teaching which he attempts to apply to the life of the Church. Each of Matthew's five books is easily relatable to the questions raised for new Christians by the precarious state of the Christian community in the world:

THE FIVE BOOKS OF MATTHEW

How am I to live as a Christian?	Book I	Discipleship	3:1-7:29
What about our leaders?	Book II	Apostleship	8:1-11:1
What is God up to in the world?	Book III	The Coming Kingdom	11:2-13:53
What about the Christian community?	Book IV	The Forgiving Church	13:54-19:1
What is it all coming to?	Book V	Judgement and God's will	19:2-26:1

> *Each of the above five teaching sections of Matthew ends with the words, "And when Jesus had finished these sayings..." The plan of the Gospel is thus easy to identify, and the scheme charted above serves as a neat outline of the book. It might be helpful for further study to have these sections clearly marked in the margins of your Bible. You might number the sections and label each with the appropriate title.*

Each of these sections begins with the story of Jesus' *deeds*. It then concludes with a collection of Jesus' *teachings*. The implication is that faith and action belong *together*.

It is also worth noting the symbolic value of having five books or sections. Matthew is presenting Jesus as the *new* Moses. Six times in the teaching half of Book 1 (5:1-7:29 - The Sermon on the Mount) Matthew has Jesus say, "It was said to you of old...but I say to you..." What follows in each case is a reinterpretation of the old Mosaic tradition. Note also these curious parallels:

- Both Moses and Jesus were spokesman for God
- Both had royalty attend their birth
- Both came out of Egypt
- Both were hidden to avoid a royal slaughter of babies
- Both were 40 days and nights in the wilderness
- Both gave their teaching on a mountain (Note that in Luke the material we call the Sermon on the *Mount* is said to have been given while Jesus was sitting on a *plain*!

Only Matthew has Jesus say that he did not come to abolish the law and the prophets (A Jewish way of referring to the Scriptures), but to fulfill them. To Matthew, a new Moses, a greater Moses has come. He is the new teacher to whom the new Christian looks for guidance in the path of faith.

C. The Coming Kingdom: A Drama in Seven Acts

We have already taken note of the five major teaching sections of the Gospel as Matthew has arranged it. When we add to that large block of material a prologue telling of Jesus' birth, and an epilogue telling of his death and resurrection, what emerges is a story told in seven sections, or, we could say, a drama in seven acts. Knowing the Jewish love of number symbolism it is possible that Matthew has consciously patterned his work so as to stimulate comparison with the seven days of creation - as if to say that in Jesus God is creating a new thing, or better, that he is bringing to fulfillment the drama inaugurated in the creation of the world.

PROLOGUE: ROYAL SAVIOUR AND MESSIAH (1:1-2:23)

Today we ask the question, "Where are you coming from?" That is, we try to get a feel for where a stranger's perspective lies so that we will know how to understand and react to him. Such would almost surely be a catechumen's first question: Who is this Jesus? Where does he come from? What is he all about? Hence Matthew begins his Gospel by telling us where Jesus was 'coming from'.

Matthew does that in good Jewish fashion with a genealogy. It is, however, a highly revolutionary one and is *not* intended to tell us about Jesus' ancestry. It is rather intended to tell us about Jesus' meaning.

The genealogy is in Matthew 1:1-17. Note the following curious features:

1. It traces Jesus' ancestry through Joseph!
2. It is artificially divided into three groups of fourteen names:

    From Abraham to David   14 generations
    From David to the exile in Babylon   14 generations
    From the exile in Babylon to Jesus   14 generations

In Hebrew, letters stood for numbers. Hence we see:

    D = 4
    A = vowels count 0
    V = 6   ⬅ *This is the way it works out in Hebrew*
    I = vowels count 0
    D = 4
        14

With this little gimmick Matthew reinforces the idea that Jesus is the promised Messiah, the son of David.

3. The list includes 5 women! Unheard of in Jewish culture! Moreover, each woman except Mary was likely not Jewish.

    Tamar (v 3)   seduced her father-in-law
    Rahab (v 5)   a canaanite prostitute
    Ruth (v 5)   a moabitess
    Bathsheba (v 6)   charmed David into killing her husband
    Mary (v 16)   mother of Jesus

Hence Matthew asserts right at the beginning that this Jesus about whom he is going to tell us is one in whose family persons of every race, sex and type belong together. It is to be a Gospel for all.

BOOK I   DISCIPLESHIP (3:1-7:29)

"Repent, for the kingdom of heaven is at hand." That is the message with which Jesus begins his ministry. While all five of Matthew's teaching sections relate to this theme, space will permit us to focus briefly on only two: we shall comment upon books I and III, those dealing with discipleship and the coming kingdom. Each organizes Jesus' teaching so as to address a pressing question in the life of the new Christian and the new Church.

    One of the critical questions might have been:

How am I, as a new citizen of this emerging kingdom, to act?

The teaching section of Book I answers this question with a clear call to a new and higher righteousness. This Sermon on the Mount, as we call it (actually collected fragments spoken on a variety of occasions), is a startling call to a revolutionary lifestyle: "Unless your righteousness exceed that of the scribes and Pharisees you will never enter the kingdom of heaven." That would take some doing. But Jesus is not a nitpicking moralist. Indeed, he is critical of such legalism. He rather probes for motives behind actions and suggests that righteousness is a matter of the heart and one's attitudes rather than the keeping of rules.

"You, therefore, must be perfect, as your heavenly Father is perfect." Sounds horrendous - as if Jesus expects us to match God's standards. The difficulty is in the translation, "perfect". It is better translated, "whole". The idea is that one is to grow into that full maturity and wholeness in which his actions, his heart and his attitudes are one. Righteousness thus ceases to be a matter of rules and encompasses one's whole being. Healthy, whole (saved), happy people are the result.

TRY THIS

Clearly Jesus is a teacher unlike any folks had ever heard. To get the spirit and flavor of what Jesus' teachings were really like, imagine the fire and brimstone of that age (not too difficult to imagine in our own age), the fears and hopes swirling in people's hearts, and the raging emotions of the new follower of Jesus who is risking everything...

1. And then quickly 'feel' your way through these excerpted sayings from the Sermon on the Mount. Let each person in your group read along silently:

    "Jesus saw the crowds and went up a hill, where he sat down. His disciples gathered around him, and he began to teach them.

    Happy are those who know they are spiritually poor...
    Happy are those who mourn...
    Happy are the meek...
    Happy are those whose greatest desire is to do what God requires...

    Happy are those who show mercy to others...
    Happy are the pure in heart...
    Happy are those who work for peace...
    Happy are those who suffer persecution...

    You are the salt of the earth...
    You are the light of the world...

    You have heard it said, Love your friends, hate your enemies. But I tell you, Love your enemies and pray for those who mistreat you...

    This is the way you should pray. Our Father...

    Do not save riches here on earth, where moths and rust destroy...instead, save riches in heaven... for your heart will always be wherever your riches are. No one can be a slave to two masters...

    You have heard that men were told in the past, Do not murder. But I tell you, Whoever is angry with his brother will be brought before the judge...

> So if you are about to offer your gift to God at the altar and you remember that your brother has something against you, leave the gift...and go at once to make peace with your brother, and then come back...
>
> You have heard it was said, An eye for an eye and a tooth for a tooth. But I tell you now, Do not take revenge on someone who does you wrong...
>
> Do not judge others so that God will not judge you... because God will apply to you the same rules you apply to others...
>
> Do for others what you want them to do for you: This is the meaning of the law of Moses and the teaching of the prophets...
>
> And the crowds were amazed at the way he taught...
>
> 2. Now let your group discuss:
>
>   How would you react if, as a new Christian, you were handed this list of sayings as a description of the lifestyle you were being called to live?

BOOK III   THE COMING KINGDOM   (11:2-13:53)

As we have seen, each of Matthew's sections alternates narrative and discourse. To be more precise, what Matthew has done is to alternate Mark and Q, that is, he has borrowed a section of Mark that tells the story of Jesus, and attached to it a body of teaching material drawn mostly from the unknown source we have called Q.

> MARK *(narrative)*
>
> +
>
> Q *(sayings)*
>
> =
>
> A MATTHEAN TEACHING SECTION

➤ *In the background of all five sections is the theme of the coming kingdom which Jesus announces at the outset of his ministry. In Matthew it is called the kingdom of **heaven** - thereby giving us a clue to the author's identity. Jews were reluctant to use the name of God, hence what is called the kingdom of God in Mark and Luke, Matthew changes to read, kingdom of heaven. By implication, the author of our first Gospel must have been a Jewish Christian.*

As in each of the teaching sections, questions of the Church and the new Christian lurk in the background:

> What is God up to in the world?
> What is this kingdom God is creating to be like?
> How shall we recognize it?

Ten times in the teaching section of Book III (chapter 13) Jesus starts out, "The kingdom of heaven is like..." He uses the illustrations of sowing seed in good and bad soils, of tiny seeds maturing into strong plants, of leaven slowly expanding through the dough, of finding unexpected treasure in a field, and so on. The message is clear: things may look meager now, but God is bringing into being a whole new day. It is to be quite unlike any other kingdom people have ever seen, certainly not like Rome. And however battered and beleaguered it may seem, "the powers of death shall not prevail against it." In the meantime, as the kingdom grows, Matthew (Jesus) calls the citizens of this new kingdom to a lifestyle radically different than that of the society around.

For the new Christian wanting it in a nutshell, Matthew (Jesus?) constructs a story of a lawyer asking Jesus which is the greatest commandment. Jesus replies:

> "You shall love the Lord your God...
>   and your neighbor as yourself." (22:34-40)

Only Matthew then has Jesus say:

> "On these two commandments depend all the law and the prophets."
> (The "law and the prophets" was a Jewish way of referring to the Scriptures.)

Above all, the new righteousness and the coming kingdom depend on practice along with preaching. It is not an age for detached theorizing:

> "Woe to you scribes, pharisees, hypocrites..."
>   (See all of chapter 23 - which appears only in Matthew)

The life of the disciple, like that of the Master, is to be one in which deed and teaching belong together.

Once again, time and space permit only a brief look at the teaching of Jesus in Matthew. The remaining teaching sections can be studied at your leisure with the background you have now acquired. Before we launch into the epilogue, the concluding act in Matthew's seven-act drama, it would be good to read the first twenty-five chapters of the Gospel. This will bring you up to the passion and resurrection narratives, the climax of the story.

READ: MATTHEW, CHAPTERS 1-25

EPILOGUE: DEATH AND RESURRECTION (26:2-28:20)

Matthew wrote to Christians who risked their lives in being publicly baptized. Their faith could cost them dearly. For such people Matthew collected the teachings of Jesus and arranged them as a call to a whole new life - and lifestyle. It goes far beyond rule-keeping and nitpicking moralism to the *heart* of the matter. It goes beyond the ordinary - love of friends, to the extraordinary - love of one's enemies. It is a call to a very radical style of living.

In Matthew's seventh and concluding section (we've looked at the introduction and the five teaching sections) he brings his Gospel to a climax. Jesus is presented as the *Lord* of his people whose authority as the Risen One extends to the ends of the earth.

In Chapter 26, after the last teaching section has concluded, Matthew takes up the narrative of Jesus' last week. The plot to kill him is hatched between Judas and the authorities (26:3-6, 14-16). Curiously, right into the middle of the betrayal story, Matthew introduces an interlude about a woman anointing the head of Jesus with some very expensive ointment. The disciples are indignant at the waste of money, but Jesus rebukes them by saying two curious things:

> "She has done a beautiful thing for me. For the poor you will always have with you, but you will not always have me."

At first that sounds as if Jesus is calloused toward the poor. But the remark probably reflects the early disciples' (who actively tried to feed the poor) awareness that when Jesus was with them they failed to recognize him as Lord. Only the woman does that. They failed to recognize the One in whose name they would later be called upon to minister to those in poverty.

Next Jesus says:

> "In pouring this ointment on my body, she has done it to prepare me for burial."

This too is likely an "after-the-fact" reflection more than a saying of Jesus. It reflects the remorse of the disciples who failed to anoint the body of Jesus in death (they fled). It also reflects their misunderstanding of his death at the time.

The beautiful irony of the whole interlude is that in being anointed, Jesus is unknowingly being proclaimed a king. This whole last section of the Gospel later climaxes in Matthew's statement of the authority of Jesus in the world, which is ironically recognized at the outset of the final events only by a poor and nameless woman.

Back to the story. The plot to arrest Jesus is laid, the Last Supper held, and Jesus goes to Gethsemane to pray with his disciples. All of the Gospels report the words of Jesus:

> "My father, if it be possible, let this cup pass from me; nevertheless not my will but yours be done."

Only Matthew, however, emphasizes that these words are repeated *three times*. Three times Jesus finds the faithless disciples sleeping, and each time he wakes them and returns to prayer. Three times the words of radical obedience are repeated (26:39, 42, 44). Jesus *chooses to be obedient* even unto death. As Jesus is arrested, Peter tries to save him by wounding a soldier with his sword, but Jesus stops him, and only Matthew reports Jesus as doing so with the words:

> "Do you think I cannot appeal to my Father, and he will at once send me more than twelve legions of angels? But how then should the Scriptures be fulfilled?"

The obedience of Jesus is radical and total, with no appeals to divine help to avoid impending suffering. (What does this say about our own frequent appeals for divine help?) In death Jesus becomes the King of Kings. So, the sign on the cross, placed there by his enemies, proclaims. What they have done in mockery, Matthew declares as Good News to the world. The King who dies becomes the risen Lord!

II. The Gospel, According to Matthew

The final words of Jesus to the disciples - that is to the whole Christian community and especially the catechumens - are spoken from a mountain (recall again Matthew's depiction of Jesus as the new Moses) in Galilee. The reaction of the disciples is telling:

> "They worshipped him; but some doubted."

Exactly the situation in the early Church! In the face of this doubt and confusion, Matthew's final presentation of Jesus is that of a majestic, authoritative Lord. Jesus has taught with authority (7:28f.), healed with authority (8:9), forgiven sins with authority (9:6,8). Now the resurrected Jesus is given authority to the ends of the earth, extended there in the mission of the disciples (all Christians) who are commanded to teach as they have been taught:

> "Go, therefore, and make disciples of all nations, baptizing them... and teaching them to observe all that I have commanded you."

No fire or revelations from heaven are to be the Gospel for the world, but precisely the words and deeds of the earthly Jesus which constitute the call to a radically new way of life. The final words are:

"I am with you always, to the close of the age."

This is not a farewell. The resurrected Jesus lives and abides in the obedience of his disciples to his teaching.

To the new Christian, aware that being a follower of Jesus could cost him dearly, the message of Matthew (Jesus) was clear. You ask how far you are to follow? What you must be prepared to risk? The answer is unmistakable: everything, including your life. In this "Age" (the Age of war, poverty, oppression, inhumanity) the disciples of the coming new Kingdom, serve their King. Because they do so - or *when* they do so - Jesus indeed becomes Lord and King with authority to the ends of the earth.

Now is the time to read the remaining chapters of Matthew which tell the passion and resurrection stories. Give special attention to the climactic note of triumph on which they end. The sevenfold drama reaches its crescendo in the story of the Risen One who is the Lord of God's new Creation.

READ: MATTHEW, CHAPTERS (26-28)

TRY THIS

The Gospel according to Matthew is a call to radical obedience as a disciple of Jesus. Jesus' teachings, always closely connected with Jesus' deeds in Matthew, are offered as a description of the new lifestyle to which the followers of Jesus are called.

1. From your reading of Matthew, recall one saying or teaching of Jesus that appears particularly radical when compared to your way of life.

2. Share your text with the group, together with your feelings about it. What practical changes in your way of doing things would be required if you were to attempt to follow the saying you have chosen?

CHAPTER 9

A UNIVERSAL SAVIOUR

THE GOSPEL ACCORDING TO LUKE

In Luke, more clearly than in any other Gospel, the One who is the hope of Israel becomes the Saviour of the whole world.

* *

IN THIS CHAPTER WE WILL LOOK AT....

I. The Gospel According to Luke
   A. Salvation history: A universal story
      1. From the beginning until John
      2. The time of Jesus and the preaching of the kingdom
      3. Resurrection and ascension: Prelude to the final era
      4. The time of the Church and the universal Gospel
   B. The structure and story of Luke
II. The Gospel, According to Luke

I. The Gospel According to Luke

The Gospel According to Luke belongs to the third stage of Christian tradition. The author tells us that himself:

"Inasmuch as many have undertaken to compile a narrative of the things accomplished among us, just as they were delivered to us by those who....

1. ⟶ from the beginning were eyewitnesses

2. ⟶ and ministers of the word,

so it seemed good to....

3. ⟶ me also

to write an orderly account for you, most excellent Theophilus." (Luke 1:1-4)

From our account of the developing tradition about Jesus in relation to the other Synoptics, the situation in Luke is not hard to understand. The oral accounts given by eyewitnesses were collected and passed on by preachers and teachers, and then finally given order and placed within a narrative by the author of Luke. Luke himself thus stands at the third stage in the development of the story of Jesus.

The earliest tradition we have concerning Luke's Gospel comes from a second century (A.D. 200) catalogue of New Testament writings known as the Muratorian Canon. In that early collection we are told that both the Gospel According to Luke and the Acts of the Apostles were written by the same author. A quick look at the opening verses of the book of Acts supports this view:

"In the first book, O Theophilus, I have dealt with all that Jesus began to do and teach..." (Acts 1:1)

Luke-Acts thus appears to have originally been a two-volume work intended to carry forward the history of God's people from the time of Israel, through the story of Jesus, and up into the period of the apostolic Church in the Gentile world.* As we shall see in a moment, the continuity of that single story about what God has done in the world is an important part of Luke's over-all message.

Luke-Acts was doubtless intended to be read as one story. We have lifted Acts out of this proper context only because we wished to set the account of the New Testament's development alongside the story Acts tells.

While there is no indication in the text of either the Gospel or the book of Acts concerning the author's identity, the earliest tradition ascribes this two-volume work to Luke, physician and companion of Paul. (See Col. 4:14; Philemon 1:24; II Tim. 4:11) Since both books display a similar style and emphasis, the claim to a single author seems justified. Moreover, the famous "we" sections of the book of Acts point toward an author who accompanied Paul on at least part of his travels, as Luke could well have done. Since a Gospel had to claim apostolic authority to gain acceptance in the Church, the supposition of Luke's association with Paul ultimately gave legitimacy to this Gospel's place in the New Testament canon.

Surprisingly little is known about this author of our third Gospel. The style and clarity of his Greek suggest that language was his native tongue. His lack of familiarity with the geography of Palestine, together with his obvious knowledge of the Greek cities of Asia Minor, suggests a Gentile Christian living in the Greek part of the Roman world.

It is also difficult to date this Gospel. Luke seems to know of the actual destruction of Jerusalem (Cp. Luke 19:43f.; and 20:21), hence a date after A.D. 70 appears likely. In light of the disparity between the picture of Paul in Acts and that in Paul's own letters, it seems unlikely that Luke knew Paul's writings, moreover, since the Pauline correspondence was in wide circulation in the early decades of the second century, the probable date of Acts is prior to A.D. 100. This means that the two-volume work, of which the Gospel was the first component, was probably written within a decade either way of the year A.D. 85.

The recipient of both volumes of Luke's work was a Gentile named Theophilus. Who this might be is difficult to say. It could have been a Gentile Christian friend for whom Luke sought to set the record of Jesus straight. Since the name 'Theophilus' is Greek for 'lover of God,' however, it could be that the name stands as a title for all lovers of God to whom the work is addressed. Beyond this simple clue our only evidence for the intended audience of the book is the broad purpose of the writing itself. Both the Gospel and the book of Acts are cast as a defense of the faith for persons who had some knowledge of Christianity's background, but who may have been troubled by accusations and charges leveled against Christians by the Gentile world. Luke writes what is called an *apology,* that is, a classic defense of the truth upon which the Gospel rests for those troubled by doubt or opposition.

Perhaps this is an appropriate place for a quick reminder about the sources and composition of Luke's Gospel. In chapter 6 we identified Mark as the earliest Gospel written, itself likely dependent upon the collection of oral and written units of the tradition we called 'pericopes'. Both Matthew and Luke appear to have used Mark as a source for their own work. Matthew and Luke in turn share a source of Jesus' sayings we have called "Q". Finally, Luke appears to have known a substantial body of tradition unknown to the other writers which, for convenience, we have labelled "L". Luke's Gospel thus is a composite of:

```
  MARK
  "Q"  (SAYINGS SOURCE)
+ "L"  (LUKE'S UNIQUE TRADITION)
─────────────────────────────
= LUKE
```

Luke obviously lived and wrote in a time when the Church needed to take a careful look at its roots. Confusion, an inevitable result of the period of oral tradition and fluid communities, had led many to undertake the writing of the story of Jesus, but evidently not to Luke's satisfaction. Having followed everything closely himself, Luke decided a more orderly account was needed that would give the Gentile Christian a clear perspective on what God had done - "the things accomplished among us," to use Luke's own words. So Luke also wrote the story. The unique insights of this Gentile author, so very different than those of Mark or Matthew, are what we now turn to consider.

A. Salvation History: A Universal Story

Luke has sometimes been called the first Christian historian. In a sense he is, though we must understand that it is a very special kind of history that Luke writes. It is what New Testament scholars call *salvation history,* that is, the history of humankind's salvation at the hands of God.

It is almost as if two histories can be carried along side by side. First, there is that world history which tells the story of human affairs in the ordinary world. But second, alongside that ordinary public history, there is the special story of God's activity in the salvation of the human race. These two stories may often intersect, but it is the latter story, the salvation story, which Luke's two-volume work is written to tell.

It is interesting to see Luke carefully document the intersection of these two histories. In chapter 2 he dates the journey of Joseph and Mary to Bethlehem (a 'salvation-event') in relation to the census when Quirinius was Governor of Syria (an ordinary historical event). In chapter 3 the ministry of John the Baptist is correlated with the reigns of Tiberius Caesar, the various rulers of Palestine, and the high-priesthood of Annas and Caiaphas in Jerusalem. With such cross-notations Luke locates salvation history in relation to the ordinary events of the public world. But having noted these intersections, it is the announcement of the Good News of what God had done in Jesus that becomes the real history occupying Luke's concern.

In Luke's mind salvation history has moved through broad epochs or stages as God worked out his plan for our salvation. In Luke 16:16 we read:

"The law and the prophets were until John; since then
the Good News of the Kingdom of God is preached."

It is all part of God's redemptive plan.

LUKE'S SALVATION HISTORY

1. ### FROM THE BEGINNING UNTIL JOHN

   A dividing point in human history has been reached because of the preaching of the Good News. The law and the prophets - the *old* story of God's dealings with his people - carry salvation history back to the birth of the human race. They tell the story of promise and hope, of failure and restoration. Now a new era has begun with the preaching of John, and with it a new chapter in the story of salvation history has been written.

2. ### THE TIME OF JESUS AND THE PREACHING OF THE KINGDOM

   With the descent of the Spirit at the time of Jesus' baptism, the era of the preaching of the kingdom of God began. To Luke this was a pivotal time in history, a time in which both the meaning of the past and the course of the future were revealed for all to see. Even though the human story will go on into the future (as the book of Acts attempts to show), Luke claims that the epoch of Jesus has been the decisive one for all of salvation history.

3. ### RESURRECTION AND ASCENSION: PRELUDE TO THE FINAL ERA

   For Luke, the transition from the era of Jesus to the ongoing history of the Church and its witness in the world (the story Acts tells) is the resurrection and ascension of Jesus. To catch the full significance of these events and the implications they bear for salvation history, we must recapitulate a theme we developed at length in our treatment of the book of Acts - the movement of the Gospel from Jerusalem to Rome. Luke's Gospel opens with Zechariah, father of John the Baptist, in *Jerusalem*. The significance of that city for Luke is evident from the fact that his is the only Gospel to begin there. In the center section of the Gospel, the part filled with the special "L" tradition, Luke highlights Jesus' critical decision to turn his face to *Jerusalem* and eventual death. Moreover, Jesus' resurrection appearances in Luke occur in and around *Jerusalem*, rather than in Galilee as in the other Synoptics. Finally, the disciples are told to wait in *Jerusalem* after Jesus' ascension until the Holy Spirit gave them power to witness to the rest of the world (Cp. Acts 1:4,8). It is all a prelude to the final epoch in which the Gospel is preached to the ends of the earth.

4. ### THE TIME OF THE CHURCH AND THE UNIVERSAL GOSPEL

   The final epoch in salvation history is that of the Church, and it centers not in Jerusalem, but in Rome. The book of Acts ends with Paul preaching openly and unhindered in Rome, which has become the focus of the Church's shifted center of gravity. Moreover, the two cities, Jerusalem and Rome, symbolize the movement of salvation history itself: it began with God's chosen people, the Jews, but in the coming of Jesus it began the transition to the far corners of the world - and to that world's capital city, Rome. What began as redemption for the Jewish people, God has turned into a universal message of Good News for the whole world.

➡️ *Another good way to catch the flavor of Luke's universal view of the Gospel is to make a brief comparison of the genealogy of Jesus in Luke's account with that of Matthew. The two accounts are found in Luke 3:23-38 and Matthew 1:1-17.*

First, look at the way the two genealogies begin:

Matthew	Luke
"The book of the genealogy of Jesus Christ, the son of David, the son of Abraham. Abraham was the father of Isaac..."	"Jesus, when he began his ministry, was about thirty years of age, being the son (as was supposed) of Joseph, the son of Heli..."
⬆️	⬆️
Here begins an attempt to show Jesus as the promised Messiah, beginning with the ancestor of the covenant, <u>Abraham</u>.	*Here begins an attempt (in reverse order) to push Jesus' roots back to the earlier era in salvation history.*

Now look at the way the two genealogies end:

Matthew	Luke
"...and Jacob, the father of Joseph and husband of Mary, of whom Jesus was born, who is called the Christ."	"...the son of Enos, the son of Seth, the son of Adam, the son of <u>God</u>."
⬆️	⬆️
Here the messianic promise bears fruit in Jesus.	*Here Jesus is kin to all people for whom God as Father is working out a universal salvation.*

> **TRY THIS**
>
> Luke's notion of 'salvation history' is a unique one. It is an attempt to look beneath the surface of ordinary history and discern the simultaneous history of what God is doing to redeem his people. The two histories often intersect and can be spoken of together. We have already noted that Luke uses these intersections to date the birth of Jesus.
>
> 1. On a blank sheet of paper draw a line down the center dividing the page into two halves. On half of the paper draw a symbolic line that represents the ordinary history of your life - not a straight line, but one that reflects the ups and downs, the circles and zig-zags of your story.
>
>   On this ordinary history-line you might also fill in a few dates or events from public world or national history that will help locate your life history.
>
> 2. On the second half of the page, draw a similar symbolic line that represents your own 'salvation history.' It could include obvious events like baptism or confirmation, but might also be drawn to symbolize experiences or events in which *you* see particular theological significance: births, deaths, marriages, friendships, crises, celebrations, etc.
>
> 3. At a few points (too many would make your paper an indecipherable scrawl) draw lines of intersection from your ordinary-history line to the salvation-history line. Dotted lines will help you keep the various lines distinct. When you have two or three such intersections clearly marked, share a few of the events in your double history with a partner in the group.
>
> In a small way, this exercise approximates what Luke was doing with the events of Jesus in his Gospel and with those of the early Church in the book of Acts.

B. The Structure and Story of Luke

Before we look at a few Lukan passages in detail, it will be helpful to get the larger picture in view. Here is a simple outline of Luke's Gospel:

AN OUTLINE OF LUKE	
I. Prologue: The New Era of the Gospel	1:1-4:13
II. Gathering Witnesses in Galilee	4:14-9:50
III. Journey to Jerusalem	9:51-19:27
IV. Passion, Resurrection, Ascension	19:28-24:53

PROLOGUE: THE NEW ERA OF THE GOSPEL

Luke's stories of the birth of Jesus are probably the best known part of the New Testament. The song of the angels and the story of the birth in a manger have long since entered the folklore of our culture. Yet neither is the key to Luke's understanding of Jesus. For that we have to look to the climax of the birth narratives in the story of Simeon (Luke 2:22-40).

According to Jewish law, the purification of a mother was to take place on the fortieth day after birth. In Luke's story, Mary and Joseph come to the temple to "do for him (Jesus) according to the custom of the law". The statement is a curious one since purification was for the mother, not the child. Obviously Luke's attention is on Jesus.

It was as Jesus' parents came into the temple courtyard for the purification rite that they encountered Simeon. The old man had been waiting at the Temple to see the revelation of God's promised Messiah - the figure from the old era waiting to see the in-breaking of the new one. He took the baby Jesus in his arms and announced to his startled parents:

> "Lord, now let your servant depart in peace, according to your word, for mine eyes have seen your salvation, which you have prepared in the presence of all peoples..."   (Luke 2:29-31)

Then comes the key statement:

> "...a light for revelation to the Gentiles, and glory to your people Israel."   (Luke 2:32)

As announced here by an old and devout Israelite, the new Gospel is to be for Jew and Gentile alike. Jesus is to be the crowning glory of the old era and the revealing light of the new.

GATHERING WITNESSES IN GALILEE

All of the Synoptics portray the ministry of Jesus beginning in Galilee and moving inexorably toward Jerusalem. The beginning was Jesus' preaching in the synagogues and villages of the Galilean countryside.

Luke's account of that beginning describes a scene in which Jesus preaches in his home town of Nazareth. In good Jewish fashion, Jesus went to the synagogue on the Sabbath "as was his custom" (4:16). Standing to read the Scripture, Jesus read from the prophet Isaiah words which Luke alone reports:

> "The Spirit of the Lord is upon me, because he has anointed me
> to preach good news to the poor. He has sent me to proclaim
> release to the captives and recovering of sight to the blind,
> to set at liberty those who are oppressed, to proclaim the year
> of the Lord's favor." (4:18-19)

The words are those of the prophet Isaiah (61:1-2; 58:6) which proclaimed the dawn of a new era. For Luke, that new era had begun in the coming of Jesus. As Jesus says, "Today this Scripture has been fulfilled in your hearing."

The reaction of the congregation in Nazareth was positive. "All spoke well of him, and wondered at the gracious words that proceeded out of his mouth." (Cp. the crowd reaction in Matthew 13:57 and Mark 6:3 where it is said they took offense at him.") Jesus goes on, however to talk about prophets lacking honor in their own country (Does this really follow from the way Luke reports the crowd response?), and recounts the Old Testament stories of Elijah and Elisha in which foreigners (Gentiles) truly recognize the word of the Lord. The implication is that those of Jesus' home territory will not understand and that the Gentiles will. At this the crowd was incensed and Jesus narrowly escaped with his life.

The importance of hearing and holding to the word of God is emphasized throughout this section of Luke. Jesus is in the process of gathering to himself witnesses who will eventually carry his word to the Gentile world. A quick comparison of Luke's account of the calling of the first disciples (5:1-11) with those of Matthew (4:18-22) and (Mark 1:16-20) confirms this Lukan emphasis on witness and response. Luke alone includes a story of the miraculous catch of fish when the disciples cast their nets at Jesus' command.

THE JOURNEY TO JERUSALEM

The journey from Galilee to Jerusalem is about sixty miles - a three or four day trek in ancient times. The incidents in this section of Luke, however, make the journey both long and significant. Much of this material is what we have labeled "L" - Luke's unique tradition that the other Synoptic writers do not share.

The opening verse is the key to understand Luke's train of thought:

> "When the days drew near for him to be received up, he set
> his face to go to Jerusalem."

Both phrases are significant. The first ("When the days drew near for him to be received up...") implies that things are going according to a plan. In this case, God's plan. As Luke sees it, salvation history is moving according to the design of God to work out the redemption of the world.

The second phrase ("...he set his face to go to Jerusalem.") is equally important. We have already commented upon the importance of the city of Jerusalem to Luke who sees it as the center of God's redemptive activity in the time before the Church. Luke alone includes in the story of the transfiguration a comment about Jesus' departure which "he was to accomplish in Jerusalem" (13:33). In setting his face toward Jerusalem and death, Jesus is acting in obedience as an agent of God's redemptive plan. The story is about Jesus, but clearly the chief actor is God.

This is confirmed for us in the three well-known parables of this section, two of which do not appear in the other Synoptics. The first parable is that of the lost sheep. It is sought and found by the shepherd. The second is that of the lost coin. It also is sought and found by its owner. In both cases the seeker is God and the one who is sought is the sinner. The emphasis is on the action of God.

The last of the three parables, the so-called parable of the prodigal son, is often misunderstood as a story about a son's repentance. While repentance does play a role in the story, it is the action of the father that is the key. He inexplicably and without repayment embraces his son and kills for him the fatted calf. The point is the same as that in the other two parables, namely, that God (the father in the prodigal story) gives cause for joy by receiving the lost son. Like the Scribes and Pharisees who could not understand Jesus, so in the story the elder son does not understand the father. In going to Jerusalem and death, Jesus becomes the agent for the Father's inexplicable grace.

PASSION, RESURRECTION, ASCENSION

We have called Luke an apology for the Christian faith. By that we mean it is a defense of the faith before charges raised among the people to whom the Gospel is addressed. Luke, the Gentile, writing for Gentiles, seeks to commend Jesus to his readers as the universal saviour of the world. But how can that be if Jesus was just another political insurrectionist judged guilty and crucified according to Roman law? In defense of the faith, Luke seeks to show Jesus an *innocent* victim who was "...crucified and killed by the hands of lawless men" (Acts 2:23).

In Luke alone does Pilate declare Jesus innocent three times (13:4; 23:14-16; 23:22). Only Luke depicts Herod as pronouncing Jesus innocent (23:6f.). We have already noted that the centurion at the foot of the cross, who in Mark and Matthew declares Jesus to be a son of God, in Luke announces Jesus' innocence (23:47). It is significant that these words do not come from Jesus' disciples or friends, but from Roman officials and army officers.

Luke is also the only one of the Gospel writers to record Jesus' dramatic word from the cross, "Father, forgive them, for they know not what they do" (23:34). Final confirmation of Jesus' innocence then comes from one of the thieves crucified at Jesus' side: "We are receiving the due reward of our deeds, but this man has done nothing wrong" (23:41). Only Luke records this. Jesus thus dies a martyr's death, falsely accused and executed, just as many of the Gentile Christians for whom Luke wrote would eventually be. Yet even here, in the tragic injustice of the crucifixion, the plan of God for the redemption of the world is working out.

Unlike the other Gospels, in Luke all of the resurrection appearances of Jesus occur in and around Jerusalem. The most significant of these is the episode that took place on the road to Emmaus, a small village about four miles outside the city.

Two of Jesus' followers were walking dejectedly along the road discussing in disappointed tones "all the things which have happened" (24:14). (Recall the introduction to the Gospel which Luke says is the record of "the things accomplished among us.") In the course of their journey the two men were joined by a stranger with whom they share their disappointment at the apparent end of their hoped-for Messiah. Jesus in turn tells the two travelers of the Scriptures concerning himself, and receives from them an invitation to join them at dinner.

In the breaking and eating of bread, the two men recognize their Lord. Many interpreters have noted the obvious parallels between this supper and the eucharistic meal of the Christian Church. In the breaking and eating of the sacramental bread in the Church, the resurrected Lord is still recognized today.

II. The Gospel, According to Luke

The final words of the Gospel confirm that in the death and resurrection of Jesus, God has completed the transition from the old era to the new. The disciples see Jesus depart from them at Bethany (just outside Jerusalem) and return to the city praising God from hearts filled with joy. The improbability of Jesus merely waving goodbye and fading from sight (24:50) seems curious, especially in light of Luke's dramatic account of Jesus' ascension in the opening verses of his second volume (Acts), but the joy of the disciples at what God has done is the heart of the matter.

This joy of the disciples (and of Luke!) is the result of what God "has accomplished among us." Salvation history has turned outward from its beginnings among the Jewish people to encompass the whole world. In Jesus, God has acted decisively for Jew and Gentile, young and old, rich and poor. Jesus does not represent a rejection of the old wine (the Jewish heritage), but its flowering and fulfillment. Nor is he subversive to Rome. He is the innocent victim of human cruelty whom God has raised in victory for the world. A new era has begun, one witnessed and proclaimed by Jesus' followers, and one recognized in the sacramental life of the Christian community. Salvation history has witnessed the working out of the redemption of God.

TRY THIS

A consistent theme of Luke's story is the universal nature of the Good News. It is a Gospel proclaimed by and for both Jew and Gentile, young and old, rich and poor. It is also an apology - a defense of the faith before those to whom the message is addressed.

1. On a blackboard or large piece of paper, brainstorm a list of potential stumblingblocks that keep the Gospel from being heard today. The scope of your discussion could be either as local as your immediate community or wide enough to include Christianity's place in the contemporary world.

2. Clarify and select two or three items from your list as the backdrop against which to ask yourselves the following:

If you were to write an apology for the faith today, what emphases would be needed in light of the discussion above?

What incidents from the Synoptics might you wish to include in order to paint a portrait of Jesus that communicates with your world?

The task this exercise envisions is really one that must go on continually wherever the Gospel is preached. The challenge in our day is probably a great deal like that which confronted Luke.

*Now is the time to read the Gospel of Luke. As per our comments at the time you were asked to read Mark, it might be a good idea to read Luke in a translation with which you are **not** familiar so as to lend a measure of freshness to its picture of Jesus.*

AN APPENDIX TO SYNOPTIC STUDY

THE PROBLEM OF THE HISTORICAL JESUS

It is impossible in a few short chapters to deal with all of the problems that arise in the study of the synoptic Gospels. Moreover, our stated objective of gaining an overview of the New Testament would be easily lost in the clutter of dealing with too many problems in detail. Before we go on to later New Testament writings, however, we are appending here a few comments about one of the problems our study has raised, the problem of the historical Jesus. We do so in order to prevent the problem from becoming a barrier to further study.

The Problem of the Historical Jesus

Many times in our study of the Synoptics you may have wondered to yourself:

>   What *really* happened?

That is, behind the theological coloring given the respective accounts of Jesus by the Gospel writers, what are the facts of the story?

Before we can approach an answer to that question it is important to see that the question itself is a modern one. People today, with the background of a scientifically oriented society, want to know in literal, factual language exactly what occurred. In Biblical times, however, precisely that interest was not as important. People then were not in the habit of writing objective historical accounts, nor did they write biography in our sense. We have already noted that the Gospels show surprisingly little interest in the usual details a modern biographer would weave into a story of Jesus.

What the Gospel writers were doing is more nearly akin to the writing of a confession of faith than to history writing in the modern sense. They were telling in story form the *meaning* of Jesus in the life of the disciple and the Church. But they were also writing *for* the Church, that is, they adapted their arrangement of the tradition to speak to the needs of the Christian communities in which they lived.

All of this presents us with a problem. We today are often fascinated with factual details and have a great need to know what '*really* happened'. Yet even the most relentless pursuit of the facts of the actual Jesus of history is forced to recognize that the Synoptic writers simply do not give us that kind of data and detail.

Over the last hundred years many scholars have tried to write an historical account of the life of Jesus using all available sources. This quest, as it has been called, has largely ended in futility. Albert Schweitzer, in his famous book, THE QUEST FOR THE HISTORICAL JESUS (written in 1910), has convincingly shown that most such stories of the life of Jesus were heavily larded with the biases and viewpoints of the author. Nor are more recent attempts free of the difficulty. The scantiness of our data means that it is far easier to read oneself into such an account than it is to get the historical Jesus out of the Gospels.

To some people this means that our Gospels are on shaky ground. But a moment's thought would make it obvious that the Christ of faith (as scholars call our theological reconstructions of Jesus) in the last analysis rests not upon a factual accounting of the life of Jesus, but upon his living presence in the Church. Not only is this true for us today, but also it was true for the writers of the Gospels themselves.

As we have seen in the Gospel According to Luke, the author acknowledges that he stands at the third stage in the process of handing down the tradition. First came the eyewitnesses. After them came the preaching of the Apostles and the spread of the faith. Only then did persons like Luke try to collect the tradition and shape it to the needs of the Church. It is difficult to say whether the writing of our Gospels occurred while eyewitnesses were still alive, but even if they were not, contact with those who had seen Jesus was not that far in the past at the time of writing. It is evident from the use of our Synoptic Gospels in the Church that confidence then existed that the Jesus of history could indeed bear the weight of the theologized Christ presented to us by the Gospel writers. The faith of the early Church was thus not so much the result of knowing 'what happened' as it was the product of knowing Christ through the eyes of the Christian community. This is exactly our position today.

This means that what actually happened will in most instances never be known. New Testament scholars are today engaged in vigorous research in the attempt to recover whatever historical data is available, but few would claim to be able to write a life of Jesus in our modern sense. The value of their research is that it subjects many of our past claims about Jesus to the hard scrutiny of historical examination, and thus helps to separate historical claims from theological ones. Much that we have assumed in the past to be history has turned out upon examination to be the theological bias of the interpreter, and in that light, much of what we have too quickly assumed about Jesus in the past must be laid to rest. A certain humility must be introduced into our discussions lest we see Jesus too much in our own image. Best of all, the research of these scholars keeps the attention of the Church focussed right where the Gospel writers intended it to be, on the Christ of faith.

TRY THIS

The problem of reading ourselves into any portrait of Jesus we might attempt to construct is one that invades all levels of New Testament study, not just that of the professional scholar. The following exercise will help you grasp what this means. It presumes the participants have by now read all three synoptic Gospels.

1. Find eight or ten pictures of Jesus and put them up around the room. They can be paintings by old masters, or modern portrayals, or whatever you can find, just so there is a good variety.

2. Ask participants to silently browse among the pictures, choosing the one they like best and the one they like least. Then go around your group and let each person indicate their choices and the reasons for them.

    As reasons are given for respective choices, incidents in the life of Jesus as told in the Gospels may be cited that are brought to mind by the various portraits.

Presumably people's tastes will differ.
So will their reasons for choosing preferences
and their memory of specific incidents
from Jesus' life which have been triggered
by viewing the pictures.

3. Now ask yourselves how much of your preferences
are the result of seeing yourselves in Jesus?
Of seeing your own sense of values captured
by the artist?

Out of this exercise should come a sense of how
easy it is to portray Jesus in our own image.
On the positive side, you may also see how any
portrayal of Jesus catches our eye precisely
because it speaks to our human needs. If so,
you will have approximated what was going on in
the writing of the Gospels themselves.

CHAPTER 10

The Church
AND THE FAITH IN THE WORLD

"It began to be clear that the end was not to come as speedily as men had thought, and that the churches might have to go on under the existing order for a long time."

E. J. Goodspeed

* *

IN THIS CHAPTER WE WILL LOOK AT....

I. The Church and the faith in the world
    A. Organization and orthodoxy - I, II Timothy, Titus
    B. The practice of the faith - James

II. The Gnostic threat: heresy and immorality - Jude, II Peter

I. The Church and the Faith in the World

First-generation Christians expected the return of Christ in their own lifetimes. With fervor and enthusiasm they anticipated the immediate fulfillment of God's promised kingdom, giving little thought to the practical details of on-going life in the Church. In their minds, the urgent need was to make ready for the return of Christ.

We have traced something of this early enthusiasm in dealing with the letters of Paul. Perhaps you recall Paul's caution to the Thessalonians about the need for patience, and his struggle with the Corinthians over the questions of marriage in the face of Christ's anticipated re-appearance. With the possibility of the present order coming to an end at any moment, there simply wasn't time to get entangled in the practical details of life in the world. Nor was there time to deal with the issues of Church organization.

But time passed, and nothing happened. As the Apostles began to die off, and initial enthusiasm waned, it gradually became clear that the Christian community must be prepared to live in the world for an indefinite time, and that the practical matters of the Church's life could no longer be neglected. Leadership was needed that was both qualified and recognized. The charitable work of the Church, particularly the offerings for the poor, had to be organized and protected from abuse. Likewise, the practical issues of living as Christians in the world needed clarification.

For example, it became evident that marriage needed to be encouraged and regulated within the life of the community. The relationships of socio-economic classes and sexes within the Church had to be worked out. Leadership had to be identified that was capable of providing an example of appropriate Christian conduct before the society, and of giving to the Church the instruction and encouragement needed for the long haul. The time had come when spiritual enthusiasm and commitment were no longer enough.

A. Organization and Orthodoxy

I, II TIMOTHY, TITUS

The transformation from enthusiastic spiritual community to established institution was a difficult one for the Church. With apostolic leadership gone, a new generation of authoritative spokesmen was needed which could give direction to the Church's struggle to live in the world. The two letters to Timothy and the one to Titus were written a half century or so after Paul's death in order to deal with these questions of Church order and discipline in the period of transition. These three letters to which we now turn are commonly called the 'Pastorals' because of their substantial concern for the pastoral leadership of the Church.

All three of the Pastorals purport to be from the hand of Paul, but as we shall see in a moment, they much more clearly reflect the situation in the period of transition described above. This would place their writing near the end of the first century or early in the second. Though their ascription to the Apostle Paul is very early (late second century), the probability is that these brief letters express the judgement of a responsible Christian leader of the early second century concerning the way the Church should be conducting its affairs. With one foot in the tradition of Paul, and the other in the world of the emerging institution, this unknown spokesman gave to the Church the sense of direction it critically required.

TIME OUT: FOR A BRIEF HISTORICAL-CRITICAL NOTE

Before we look in brief detail at the Pastorals themselves, it will be important that we not skip lightly over the problem raised by our statement that the Apostle Paul was probably not their author. Since this might trouble readers unacquainted with the historical/critical study of the Bible, it is best that we take a look at the problem head-on. A way to do that might be to comment briefly upon both the ancient practice of attributing books to well-known persons, as well as the specific reasons for proposing an unknown author for the Pastoral letters.

When we looked at the book of Ephesians, we commented upon the practice in the ancient world of attributing authorship to a well-known person in whose tradition the actual author honestly felt he stood. This was not an attempt to deceive (the actual author may have been well known to his readers), but a way of saying that the ideas expressed were truly not the author's own. They were those of the famous person to whom the book was attributed. **Pseudepigraphy,** *as this literature is called, was common in the New Testament world, including the early Church.*

Whether the Pastorals should be so regarded is an important question for our understanding of the development of the New Testament. The reasons for suggesting that these three short letters were written by an unknown Christian leader of the early second century can be summarized as follows:

1. *The earliest collections of Paul's letters do not include the Pastorals. It is not until late in the second century that there is evidence associating these letters with the Pauline corpus.*

2. *The style and language of the Pastorals differ markedly from the Pauline letters we read earlier, while among themselves they show great similarity. It is significant that their language and vocabulary are much more like that of the great Christian writers of the second century than that of Paul.*

3. *In both theology and Church organizational concern, the Pastorals reflect a far different situation than that of Acts and the Pauline letters. For example, "faith" has now generally become "the faith" (Cp. I Tim. 3:9; 4:1; II Tim. 4:7). What for Paul was a style of relationship has now become a body of doctrine. Heresy, though a problem from the beginning, is now a highly developed and widespread threat to the Church. Moreover, the theological controversy is no longer primarily the one with the judaizers as in the Pauline period, but with a highly developed synthesis between Christianity and Greek philosophies.*

4. *Paul's view of the leadership of the Church was largely functional - certain things needed doing and required persons willing to undertake the tasks. The Pastorals, however, reflect a developed clergy which is distinct from the laity and holding positions of ordained authority in the Church.*

5. *Finally, in spite of his counsel to the Thessalonians for patience as they awaited Christ's return, Paul's outlook always remained one of expectancy toward Christ's quick return. The Pastorals, on the other hand, are obviously directed toward the Church's life in the world over an indefinite period. It is difficult to see how the atmosphere could have changed so markedly without the passage of considerable time.*

No one of these arguments taken alone would be decisive. Other explanations could be found for many of them taken singularly, but together they make attribution of the Pastorals to Paul extremely difficult. In fact, the sum of them suggests that these letters were written fifty or sixty years after Paul by a leader attempting to speak a genuine word of Paul for his own day. As such, the Pastorals are an important chapter in the unfolding story of the Church and the faith in the world.

I TIMOTHY (II TIMOTHY, TITUS)

The two major concerns of I Timothy and Titus are: ecclesiastical organization and the threat of heresy (II Timothy is primarily concerned with the latter). Both men were younger associates of Paul known to us from Paul's letters and the story in Acts. The two letters to Timothy are addressed to him at Ephesus, while the one to Titus places him on the island of Crete. A brief look at the opening chapters of I Timothy will serve as our introduction to these Pastoral letters.

THE STRUCTURE OF I TIMOTHY	
I. Warnings Against Heresy	1:1-20
II. Worship and Church Order	2:1-3:13
III. Instructions for Pastors	3:14-6:21

The first letter to Timothy begins with a stern warning against those who occupy themselves with "myths, and endless genealogies which promote speculation..." (1:4). While the exact nature of these heresies cannot be determined now, it is probable that they represented a form of Jewish legalism (I Tim. 1:9) that had been influenced by gnostic philosophy.* Rigorous practices of self-denial and highly speculative mythology swirled everywhere in the Mediterranean world of that day, and doubtless attracted many Christians when such philosophies were given a connection with the Old Testament heritage. The fact that our author singles out the teachers of this heresy by name is perhaps an indication of the seriousness with which he viewed this distortion of the faith.

The second section of I Timothy provides instructions for public worship together with the appropriate qualifications for those in positions of leadership. Prayers are to be offered by *men*, while women maintain silent modesty and good deeds. The exclusion of female leadership in public worship appears to be a stern reversal of the earlier freedom for all to share in public prayer. (Cp. Paul's attitude in I Corinthians 11:2-16 where the conditions under which women lead in worship are structured and regulated, but no prohibition is suggested. Note also that most scholars consider I Corinthians 14:33b-36 to be a later insertion that obviously interrupts the flow of thought and thus not from the hand of Paul.)

The qualifications for the offices of bishop (also called *elders*: leaders in a local church) and deacon suggest the need for mature leadership that embodied the Church's stance in the world. Both moral character and family relationships are to be taken into account when choosing persons for these offices.

The remainder of the letter of I Timothy consists of encouragement and instructions for pastors, including personal advice for Timothy in relation to various people in his congregation. It ends with the exhortation to avoid the "godless chatter and contradictions of what is falsely called knowledge" (6:20) that have caused many to miss the mark.

> *Now is the time to read I Timothy. You may also wish to read II Timothy and Titus, though we shall not comment upon them in detail. Their similarity to I Timothy should be obvious to any reader.*

B. THE PRACTICE OF THE FAITH
JAMES

The letter of James undoubtedly arose out of the actual needs of the expanding and consolidating Church. Both the letters of Paul and the Synoptic Gospels implied the direct connection between faith and action which constantly confronted new Christians and new churches, a subject which James now addresses directly. The need for specific, concrete guidance in actual life-situations was an ongoing one as the Church developed.

* *If you have lost your grip on the term gnosticism, you may want to review our discussion of it on page 26.*

Unfortunately, few documents in Christian history have given rise to as wide a variety of interpretations as this brief letter. Almost nothing is known of its origin or intended recipients, and many have even doubted its place in the canon. Eusebius, the fourth century Church historian, indicated that its position was widely questioned in his day. Martin Luther is often quoted as calling James an "epistle full of straw", not because he disliked its moral exhortations, but because of its lack of theological depth.

Luther also doubted the tradition that the book was written by James, the brother of Jesus. Though the book does not claim this, the tradition that Jesus' brother wrote the book is an old one and was eventually accepted by the Church. The difficulty is that the letter shows no interest in the earthly Jesus, strange if its author was his brother, and also that it evidences a Greek form and style that seem unlikely for someone from Nazareth.

The fact is that we do not know who the James referred to in the letter really is. Nor are we confident of the letter's recipients. They are called the "Twelve Tribes of the Dispersion," but the letter is not addressed to Jews. Apparently Christians could be referred to as the Dispersion, and the author has thus intended a general letter addressed to scattered Christians everywhere

The letter of James has two obvious concerns: (1) the author's conviction that wealth is evil, and (2) the relationship of faith and good works. The fact that these concerns emerge out of a loosely strung together series of sayings has led some commentators to suggest that James was originally a kind of street-corner sermon delivered by an itinerant Christian preacher. The form and outlook of the book are characteristically Jewish, though the concern for the evils of wealth suggests the time late in the first century when the relationships between rich and poor in the Church had become a matter of open controversy.

Many commentators have charged James with misunderstanding the nature of the Christian faith. His argument that faith without works is dead (2:14-26) is often cited as a direct challenge to Paul's notion of justification by faith alone. Especially problematical is James' use of Abraham and Rahab as Old Testament figures saved by their works rather than by faith. Paul had used Abraham as an example of just the opposite, faith, while the book of Hebrews uses Rahab the same way. The letter of James may reflect a time when Paul's doctrine of justification by faith had become a religion without morality, and hence in need of a corrective exhortation to concrete action in the world.

READ: JAMES *Since the letter of James is a loosely strung together series of moral exhortations, no outline or structural picture is necessary in order to read it. Aside from its opening epistolary address, it shows few signs of being a letter in the traditional sense. It is better read as a series of moral injunctions.*

TRY THIS Though the situations are obviously only roughly analogous, it might help you understand the critical nature of the issues being dealt with in the Pastorals and James if you were to try to imagine yourself and a group of other

Christians forming a new congregation in your community. If you can set aside the accumulated patterns of your church or denomination for a moment, try to envision what problems of leadership and organization your group would face.

1. On a blackboard or large piece of paper, list a few of the leadership positions you feel you would need in order for your new congregation to function and carry out its mission. Three or four such positions might be identified.

2. Break your large group into smaller ones, giving each small group the assignment of spelling out the implications of one of the leadership positions the whole group decided were necessary. For example, if your group decides that your new congregation needs:

   a pastoral counselor
     a preacher
       an administrator
         an educational expert
           etc.

   then let each small group represent one of these positions. Ask the small groups to spell out two things in relation to their assigned leadership position:

   a. What *personal* (*not* professional) qualifications should this individual possess?
   b. What authority should he or she have in the Church?

3. When the small groups have a handle on the above, let them share their consensus with the entire group. You might also ask yourselves where such persons could be found and how your congregation could enlist their help.

Though the analogy is a rough one, the exercise above approximates what was going on all across the early Church. The Pastoral letters were written to address these issues and call for a consensus among the congregations. Given the rapid change going on in our society today, and consequently the need to re-think old patterns of church organization and leadership, it is conceivable that in the near future the above could turn out to be more than an academic exercise!

II. The Gnostic Threat: Heresy and Immorality

By the second or third decade of the second century, the difficulties of the emerging Church brought it close to crisis. So much time had now passed without the expected return of Christ that it became increasingly difficult to maintain the promise. The growing complexities of Church organization brought disputes over authority and practice within congregations, as well as among the various geographical sections of the Church. Most serious of all were the growing inroads of gnosticism and other heretical versions of the faith. By the time of the letters of Jude and II Peter, the situation had reached the flashpoint.

JUDE

The letter of Jude was evidently written by a concerned Christian in the second century who was distressed by the gnostic influence in the Church. He relates that he had planned a longer letter on the subject of "our common salvation", but that news had reached him of persons who had secretly gained entrance into the Christian community and were perverting it by teaching that moral conduct was of little consequence to those who had been saved by the grace of God.

What the author - and we simply do not know who he was - evidently had in view was the teaching of some gnostics that all physical matter is intrinsically evil, and that the Christian faith therefore relates only to the concerns of the spirit. Such gnostics believed that what one does in the body is of little consequence and has no effect on one's spiritual condition. So concerned was Jude that he poured out a vehement blast against all such false teachers, leaving the longer letter on the subject of salvation forgotten in the heat of battle.

Though the tradition has identified Jude as the brother of Jesus, there is nothing in the letter to suggest that this is the case. The style of the letter actually reflects a much later period when the author could look back on the time of the apostles (v. 17) and evoke its memory in the Church. This, together with the rather developed form of the gnostic threat against which the letter rails, makes a date in the first half of the second century the most probable.

The most interesting aspect of the letter of Jude is the emergent catholicism it exhibits. The letter speaks of the "faith once for all delivered to the saints," as if faith had by now become a body of doctrines to be accepted as authoritative. It also uses liturgical language that reflects a developing institutional life. Jude tells his readers to "pray in the Holy Spirit; keep yourselves for the love of God; wait for the mercy of our Lord Jesus Christ" - an obvious liturgical development of trinitarian language. The closing benediction of the letter, one of the best known such doxologies in the New Testament, is so different in style than the rest of the letter that it too suggests the writer has borrowed from the liturgical practice of his congregation.

II PETER

The letter we call II Peter was probably the last part of our New Testament written.* It reflects the same concern with the gnostic threat as does Jude, and indeed, it uses the letter of Jude wholesale as its second chapter. The principal difference in the two letters is the greater emphasis in II Peter on reaffirming the expected return of Christ. By the time II Peter was written, that hope had obviously been given up by many people in the Church.

II Peter is also another example of pseudepigraphy - the practice of placing an apostle's name on a letter intended to speak his word to a later day. By the second century the name of Peter had gained such stature in the Church that it was widely used as a pseudonym in Christian writing. Both the author's use of Jude, and his obvious concern for the later developments of gnostic influence, suggest that the Apostle Peter could not have authored the work. The strong emphasis on the reaffirmation of the Parousia, for which there was no need yet in Peter's day, confirms this judgement.

Many commentators, including those in the early Church, have doubted the canonical value of II Peter. We have no mention of it until late in the second century, and much of the Church did not use it until the fourth century when it came to be believed that Peter wrote it. While both II Peter and Jude may lack the religious value of other New Testament works, they are both important witnesses to the crisis experienced by the Church in the transition from spiritual community to complex institution. Moreover, their insistence on sound theology as a basis for sound living speaks to a universal need in human experience.

READ: II PETER

Now is the time to read II Peter. In the process of doing so, you might compare its second chapter with the letter of Jude.

TRY THIS

Though we have discussed it now a number of times, GNOSTICISM is a hard item to get a handle on. It is important to do so, however, because gnostic-like ideas are still prevalent in Christian communities today just as they have always been.

1. The chart below lists a few gnostic ideas side by side with those the early Church viewed as orthodox. Allow time for participants to study the chart sufficiently to get at least a beginning grasp on the opposing sets of ideas. The group leader can perhaps clarify the summary statements, but an extended discussion of the respective ideas should wait until later.

Though Jude and II Peter were likely the last New Testament books written, we are considering them here in order to carry through the story of the emerging Church to its New Testament conclusion. In a moment we shall go back and pick up the Church's reaction to growing persecution (Hebrews, I Peter, Revelation), together with its final statement of the Good News (the writings of John).

GNOSTICISM	ORTHODOXY
The material world is evil, and was created by lesser beings.	God created the material world and saw that it was very good.
Spiritual realities are all that count.	Both the body and the spirit are of ultimate value.
The soul is immortal, and never dies; the body is a prison to be shucked off.	Only God is immortal; the resurrection of the body is God's re-creating gift.
Salvation is to live in spiritual enlightenment; it is an escape from this world to a higher realm.	Salvation is trusting God with your whole self; it is to live in the world without alienation from God or others.

2. Using this partial list of gnostic and orthodox beliefs as a guide to understanding these two outlooks, allow your group to think its way through the following list of concepts to see if they can anticipate how a gnostic and/or an orthodox Christian might have viewed them. A chart could be drawn on a blackboard of large piece of paper that would look like this:

	GNOSTICISM	ORTHODOXY
a. Marriage:		
b. End of the world:		
c. Death		
d. World hunger:		
e. Suffering of Jesus		
f. Old Testament:		

Discuss each of the above ideas and see if you can follow the logic of each position to determine how they might have viewed these topics.

3. After filling in the chart above as a means of checking out the group's understanding of gnostic ideas, let your group discuss the most significant

issue:

> Where do you see the influence of
> gnostic-like ideas in the Church
> today?

The time and effort spent by the later writers of the New Testament in dealing with the threat of gnosticism might give us pause for thought in light of its persistent influence throughout the history of the Church.

CHAPTER 11

THE PERSECUTION OF THE CHURCH

"Eighty and six years have I served him, and he has done me no wrong. How can I blaspheme my King who has saved me?"

                        Polycarp, Bishop of Smyrna A.D. 155
                        (on the day he was burned at the stake)

* *

IN THIS CHAPTER WE WILL LOOK AT.....
I. The persecution of the Church
II. Letters of comfort and encouragement
    A. Suffering for Christ - I Peter
    B. The pioneer and perfector of faith - Hebrews
    C. He who overcomes - Revelation

I. The Persecution of the Church

The possibility of suffering and persecution threatened the Church right from the beginning. The catalogue of Paul's suffering for his faith at the hands of both Jews and Gentiles, together with his death in the persecutions of Nero, were a fate shared by Christians everwhere. The Synoptic interest in the suffering of Jesus, particularly in the Gospel of Mark, bears ample testimony to the climate of fear under which the Church struggled.

The official policy of the Roman government was one of tolerance toward local religions. The polytheistic religion of the Empire made the inclusion of new gods and new religions a simple matter. All Rome asked was that local populations formally acknowledge the official gods of Rome as an act of loyalty to the Empire, after which they were free to practice their local beliefs without interference.

Simple as this demand was, however, it was more than the monotheistic faith of the Jewish people would permit. They refused to worship the gods of Rome. Finally a compromise was worked out in which the special position of the Jewish people was recognized by Roman authorities in return for a pledge of loyalty to the Empire. So long as Christianity was viewed as a sect of Judaism, it too flourished under the protection afforded by the special Jewish situation. By the time of the Neronian persecutions, however, the growing recognition of Christianity as a religion distinct from Judaism left it without the status of a legalized religion.

In the latter half of the first century, Christians were sporadically required to acknowledge the Roman gods and threatened with banishment, torture, or death if they refused. Serious outbreaks of persecution occurred twice during this period, under Nero in the year A.D. 64, and later under Domitian in about A.D. 95. It is probable that the persecutions of Nero centered primarily in the city of Rome, and, according to the tradition, it was at that time that both Peter and Paul perished by Roman hands.

The persecutions of Domitian thirty years later appear to have centered in Asia Minor rather than Rome. They were probably precipitated by the growing demand for worship of the emperor, a practice which began in the eastern part of the Empire and gradually spread west. Earlier this emperor-worship had been a sporadic affair, more an expression of loyalty to the state than a true divinizing of the emperor, but finally Domitian insisted on claiming divine honors for himself and sponsored local cults of priests to coerce compliance with the demand. Once again the special case of the Jews was given official recognition, but Christians were left with the demand to participate. As Christians refused, the blood began to flow.

II. Letters of Comfort and Encouragement

Three books in our New Testament grew out of these persecutions endured by the Church - I Peter, Hebrews, and the Revelation to John. Each in its own way offered to the Church comfort and encouragement in the face of suffering. In all three books it is to the figure of Jesus that the author turns as the foundation on which to rest his call to the Church to stand fast.

Like so many of the books in the New Testament, the three we are now considering were written by authors who are anonymous to us. Though we shall look at the question of authorship and date in relation to each book in more detail shortly, the probability is that all three originated in the persecutions of Domitian in A.D. 95-96, and were written by leaders in the Church unknown to us today. We know that Domitian's harassment of Christians was particularly severe in Asia Minor, to which both I Peter and Revelation are specifically addressed. This may have been the backdrop against which the book of Hebrews was written as well. Since each of the three books is such a different response to the suffering of the early Christians, each is worth looking at individually.

A. Suffering for Christ

I PETER

Until modern times no objections were raised to this praise-worthy letter having been written by the Apostle Peter. The robust, sermonic character of the letter has traditionally been thought in perfect character with what is known of Peter, and no one doubted his authorship.

In recent years, however, several cogent objections have surfaced that may mean a revision in our estimate of the letter's significance and origin. For one thing, it is written in excellent Greek, hardly likely for an Aramaic-speaking Palestinian. The fact that Silvanus acted as secretary for the author (Cf. 5:12) may overcome this objection, unless this Silvanus is to be identified with the Silas of the book of Acts (Acts 15:22,27), for he too was a native Palestinian.

A more severe objection to Petrine authorship is the fact that the book evidences nothing like the acquaintance with the historical Jesus such as one might expect from a man like Peter. The author of this letter indicates he personally saw Jesus' suffering (5:1), yet according to the Gospels Peter fled and presumably saw nothing.

Finally, there is the question of the recipients of the letter. They are listed as exiles in the Dispersion of Asia Minor, and are obviously undergoing persecution for their faith. Yet no persecution of Christians occurred in Asia Minor until the time of Domitian, thirty years after Peter died by the hand of Nero in Rome.

Such arguments are not, of course, decisive. With this book, as with so many others, we may never know who penned it. What we do know is that this short letter is one of the gems of the New Testament, written to suffering Christians in Asia Minor, encouraging them in their faith.

It may also be that the structure of I Peter offers a clue to the origin of the book and the intent of its author. Many commentators have noted that following the opening salutations there is what appears to be a baptismal sermon addressed to believers:

```
               THE STRUCTURE OF I PETER

    I.  Salutations                       1:1-2
   II.  Baptismal Sermon                  1:3-4:11

           At 4:11 there is an obvious conclusion,
           after which comes a final section:

  III.  Encouragement to Endure           4:12-5:11
```

One key to understanding this structure is to note that prior to 4:11 persecution is viewed as a real possibility, while after that point the readers are actually undergoing a "firey ordeal". The very plausible suggestion has been made that the opening section (1:3-4:11) is a baptismal sermon, a copy of which has been sent to Christians undergoing persecution in Asia Minor, with a note attached by the author who wished to encourage these people in the midst of their ordeal. The fact that baptism, in which the convert publicly identified himself with the Christian community, was the point at which the new Christian needed instruction in the risk he was undertaking makes the suggestion a particularly insightful way of understanding the book.

➤ READ: I PETER

Now is the time to read I Peter. Give special attention to the change in climate after 4:11. You might also note the similarity between I Peter 2:21-25 and Isaiah 53.

B. The Pioneer and Perfector of Faith

HEBREWS

A second piece of encouragement to Christians enduring persecution for their faith, and another of the highpoints of the New Testament, is the book of Hebrews. Not a letter in the proper sense of the term (the book contains only the briefest epistolary notations in the final verses), Hebrews is really a sophisticated and eloquent sermon by a Christian who offers concern and guidance to those suffering for their faith.

Less is known about the origin, the date, or the recipients of Hebrews than of any other New Testament book. It had to have been written before the year A.D. 96, because in that year Clement, the Bishop of Rome, quotes it in a letter to Corinth. Yet the thrust and content of Hebrews seem to imply that its author was a second-generation Christian (Cf. 2:3) writing late in the first century. Rome has been suggested as the probable destination, both because of the quote by Clement and because of the brief note in 13:24 offering the greetings of "those who come from Italy." It was clearly written to Christians, though the intended readers may have been of Jewish background.

Though the tradition has ascribed Hebrews to Paul, there is really no evidence for authorship on the part of Paul or anyone else. Origen of Alexandria (A.D. 185-254) summed up the puzzlement of the early Church with the simple comment that, "The author is known to God alone". While the supposition of Pauline authorship eventually won a place for Hebrews in the canon, the probability is that it gained wide acceptance in the early Church primarily because of its excellence in encouraging Christians to stand fast for their faith.

The author of Hebrews is eloquent in style, and obviously practiced in the methods of Biblical interpretation of his day. In good rabbinic style he uses an old Scripture (Psalm 110) as the basis around which to weave his own comments for his own day. The book of Hebrews is not, however, an easy one for English readers. The sacrificial and priestly terminology the author uses is often difficult for us to follow. Special attention should thus be given to the chart below which clarifies the structure of the book and follows its central flow of thought.

```
              THE STRUCTURE OF HEBREWS

    I.   Prologue: God's final word          1:1-2
   II.   Jesus' Superiority                  1:3-4:13
  III.   Jesus, the True High Priest         4:14-10:39
   IV.   O. T. Examples of Faith             11:1-39
    V.   Jesus, The Pioneer of Faith         12:1-17
   VI.   Exhortation to Faithfulness         12:18-13:17
  VII.   Closing Greetings                   13:18-25
```

Because of the difficulty reading Hebrews presents, it might be helpful if we summarize the author's argument. It is a complex one intended to re-kindle enthusiasm on the part of Christians suffering persecution. Throughout the book the writer is keenly aware of what another major persecution could do to a spiritually weakened Church.

The writer of Hebrews thinks in terms of a heavenly reality and an earthly copy of that reality, as if the earth were the shadow of the substance above. "By faith", he says, we grasp the higher realities which God has made known to us in many ways throughout history. Now God has spoken to us his final word in his Son.

The major theme throughout Hebrews is that what has been revealed to us earlier through the prophets is but a shadow of the glory revealed to us in Jesus. His superiority over angels, and over Moses, is argued as a prelude to his acclamation as the supreme High Priest. Jesus is called a priest after the order of Melchisidek, a cryptic designation taken from Psalm 110:4 and applied to Jesus as a symbol for a priesthood that gains its validity from total conformity to the will of God. As such, Jesus becomes the ultimate mediator of the ancient promise.

The opening verses of Chapter 12 are often isolated by Christian readers as eloquent testimony to Jesus who is the "pioneer and perfector of our faith, who for the joy that was set before him endured the cross, despising the shame, and is seated at the right hand of the throne of God (12:2)." This is the climax of the author's argument, encouraging his readers to likewise stand fast and endure to the end. For those who do, the reward will be the same exaltation given to Jesus.

READ:
HEBREWS

You may want to read the entirety of Hebrews and, if so, we encourage you to use a good modern translation. If not, you might try reading the following as a summary of the author's argument:

Chapters 1-2   God's final, superior word
4:14-5:10   Jesus, the supreme High Priest
Chapter 11   Examples of men of faith
Chapters 12-13   Encouragement to stand fast

---

c. he who overcomes

THE REVELATION TO JOHN

No book in the New Testament has occasioned such controversy as the Revelation to John. As the source of endless speculation about the end of the world, it has spawned countless movements within Christendom to apply its prophecies to every troubled period in western history, including the twentieth century. Wars, rumors of wars, earthquakes, political upheavals, and a multitude of other cataclysmic events in human history have stimulated the speculators to in turn incite thousands of people to quit their jobs, flee to the mountains, and await the end of the world - all because of a purported prediction found in the book of Revelation! Every impending war has been called the battle of Armageddon, and every dictator who arises, the Antichrist. Nineteen hundred years of such fanciful speculation has produced nothing, but continues unabated in our own day.

The fact is that from the middle of the second century onward, Revelation has been a disputed book in the Church. Knowing almost nothing of the book's origin or setting, and with the circumstances that occasioned it quickly lost from memory, substantial portions of the early Church refused to use the book at all. Some rejected it as late as the 14th century A.D. The cryptic language of the book, together with the aura of the bizarre which has been created by the speculators predicting the world's demise, has meant that even today the book is a closed one for many Christians. Yet with a little historical/critical background, we should be able to appreciate the book as one of the Church's most dramatic statements of Christian liberty in the face of Roman persecution.

Two factors must be kept constantly in mind as we try to understand Revelation: (1) the specific first-century situation to which the book is addressed, and (2) the nature of the apocalyptic language in which it is written. Let's look at both factors.

The book of Revelation is addressed to Christians in Asia Minor who are suffering persecution for their faith. We have already noted that the first Roman persecutions - those under Nero in A.D. 64 - centered largely in Italy. It was not until the reign of Domitian (A.D. 81-96) that significant persecution occurred in Asia Minor, hence most Biblical scholars date Revelation in Domitian's reign.

Domitian was the first Roman Emperor to make an issue of emperor worship. It had existed sporadically in the eastern part of the empire for some time, but for political as well as personal reasons, Domitian spread the cult. He saw it as a way of consolidating his far-flung empire, and so required public sacrifices to himself. He ordered himself called "Our Lord and Our God", and even referred to his food and couch as sacred. Death was the penalty for refusal to comply.

The reaction of Christians was varied. Some renounced their faith outright, while others performed the sacrifices without believing what they were doing. Many Christians faced death with a quiet resolution that the Romans found both amusing and incomprehensible. Still others, perhaps a very few, raised cries of defiant protest, and declared that God's righteous wrath would descend like a consuming fire upon the harlot city which had violated the peoples of the earth.

One such Christian was a leader of the Church in Asia Minor by the name of John. Exiled to the island of Patmos (25 miles off the coast of Asia Minor) for his faith, this John wrote to his beleaguered fellow-Christians in the cities of Asia Minor to encourage them to stand firm to the end. His message was that their suffering would be brief because God was about to establish his kingdom on the earth forever.

The Revelation to John was thus written to a specific group of Christians, caught in a very specific and temporary crisis, encouraging them with visions of "what must *soon* take place" (1:1,3). The author plainly tells us that what he is writing is for his own time: "Do not seal up the words of the prophecy of this book, for the time is near...Behold I am coming soon" (22:10-12). Far from being visionary speculation about the far distant future, Revelation was written to encourage embattled Christians in the days immediately ahead.

The second factor we must understand before reading Revelation is the nature of its apocalyptic outlook and language. Though it is strange and even bizarre to modern ears, the language of apocalyptic literature was well-known to both Christians and Jews of the first century.

> *Apocalypticism is another of those items on which it is easy to lose your grip. If the term has faded for you a bit, go back and review our comments on pp. 23-24.*

The word "apocalyptic" means to *reveal* or to *unveil,* and is used of literature which speaks of the coming New Age as the end of history. What is meant is not the time when history grinds to a halt, but that time when history reaches its appointed end or goal - that is, when God's eternal kingdom is established on the earth.

Speculation about this end or goal of the world was very popular in Jesus' day, and we have already commented upon its influence in the Synoptic Gospels. Apocalyptic books were common in the first century, and most are written in the visionary language typical of Revelation. Such writing was a kind of "code", easily understood by Christians (or Jews) and yet nonsense to the Romans. Since most of the cryptic symbols were taken from the Old Testament, the writer of Revelation had a ready vehicle with which to denounce the wickedness of Rome in a language only his fellow-Christians could understand.

Such writing was always born in crisis (Cp. Ezekiel 37-39, Isaiah 24-27, Joel, Zechariah, Zephaniah, and Daniel 7-12 in the Old Testament), and always proclaims a revelation of what God was about to do to save his people from the evil situation. Once this character of apocalyptic writing is understood, and once the specific historical situation to which it is addressed is identified, what had previously been only an enigmatic puzzle now becomes a dramatic testimony to the blazing hope of the persecuted people of God.

LETTERS TO THE SEVEN CHURCHES

Revelation is addressed to the "seven churches that are in Asia" (1:4). The writer identifies himself as "your brother", and also as one who has received from the Lord a prophecy or revelation for the churches. Who this John is we do not know, though he writes as if he is well known to his readers. Though the tradition has identified him with John, the son of Zebedee, the Greek style, the circumstances of the writing, and the theological viewpoint make this highly unlikely. We know from other sources that an Elder John was a prominent figure in the Asian churches, but no positive evidence exists to link him to this book. It is perhaps best to view the author as an anonymous prophet of some stature in the churches to which he writes.

The seven churches are identified by name: Ephesus, Smyrna, Pergamum, Thyatira, Sardis, Philadelphia, and Laodicea. The map on the next page will help you get them located:

THE SEVEN CHURCHES OF REVELATION

While the book of Revelation is not a letter in the usual sense, it does open with letters to the seven churches. The order in which the churches are listed is the sequence in which one would visit them using existing roads. The symbolic use of the number seven (7) throughout the book suggests, however, that these seven may stand for the whole Church.

➤ *The use of the symbolic number 7 simply cannot be overlooked. There are seven churches, seven lampstands, seven seals, seven trumpets, seven golden bowls, etc. In Old Testament symbolism the*

> *number 7 was the perfect number, the number which stood for completeness or totality. Its use throughout Revelation suggests that John is telling the **whole** story, holding nothing back. Throughout Revelation the use of number symbols is prevalent.*

The letters to the seven churches ground the book of Revelation in actual human history. You may want to read them as you follow the comments below. They are in chapters 1-3.

1. **EPHESUS** — One of the leading churches of the Christian world. It was the capital of the Roman province of Asia. The principal heresy weakening the churches was probably Gnosticism, whose adherents claimed the liberty to compromise with emperor worship. Ephesian enthusiasm for Christ had obviously begun to wane.

2. **SMYRNA** — A commercial rival of Ephesus. The church here is told to endure because persecution will last only ten days - that is, for a very short time. Endurance will bring a "crown of life."

3. **PERGAMUM** — A staunch ally of Rome, this city erected a temple in 29 B.C. to honor Augustus Caesar. Later the temple became the center of emperor worship, and is doubtless the "throne of Satan" referred to in the letter. Balaam was an Old Testament character who advocated compromise (Numbers 22-24).

4. **THYATIRA** — A flourishing dye industry supported this city. "Jezebel" - an unknown woman - was apparently leading Christians astray. The phrase, "...who know the deep things of Satan", is likely a reference to the Gnostic idea that *all* human experience was to be explored and then accepted or rejected.

5. **SARDIS** — The Church here was in as much danger from the city's notorious lifestyle as it was from persecution. The "book of life" is a reference to the register of the citizens in the heavenly kingdom spoken of in Exodus 32:32. Remember, it is symbolism.

6. **PHILADELPHIA** — This city was strategically located on the trade routes from the coast to the interior of Asia Minor. Those who endure are told they will be made pillars of the temple of God, and have identifying names written upon them. Names written on doorposts were a common means of identification in Roman cities, and here symbolize the clear stand taken by those who endure.

7. **LAODICEA** — In A.D. 60 an earthquake destroyed this city, but it recovered without outside help. Its wealth came from banking and the processing of a fine black wool. White-robed Christians (figuratively speaking) would thus stand out from their neighbors with unmistakable clarity. The reference to being hot or cold conveys the same idea. Lukewarm fenceriders are to be cast out.

Revelation alternates visions of judgement and despair with those of victory and hope. The unmistakable message throughout the book is that of the ultimate triumph of God over the forces of darkness and evil. The opening of the seven seals (chapters 4-7), the blowing of the seven trumpets (chapters 8-11), and the pouring out of the seven bowls of God's wrath (chapters 15-16) are all symbols used to describe the terrible woes that will come upon the earth because of the reign of evil. The crowning blow will be the appearance of the Antichrist who demands the worship that is due to God alone (chapters 12-14). His coming will also be a sign that the end is near, that the final triumph of God has begun.

The Antichrist is not named in Revelation, but we are told that readers with understanding will know who he is from the number of his name (13:18). His number is 666.

The meaning of the riddle is clear when we remember that in the ancient world numbers could stand for letters. Any person's name thus has a numerical equivalent. For example, in English, if we let "A" equal "1", "B" equal "2", and so on, the following is possible:

$$J = 10$$
$$O = 15$$
$$H = 8$$
$$N = 14$$
$$\overline{47}$$

Thus the name "John" bears the numerical equivalent 47. The beauty of the device is that 47 could be the numerical equivalent of countless letter combinations, hence we have a cryptic way of referring to someone we do not wish to name.

The mystery of chapter 13 comes clear as soon as we realize that the name with the numerical value of 666 in Greek is:

NERO CAESAR!

In chapter 13, this first beast (Nero) gives his authority to a second (Domitian). They were, of course, the first two emperors to persecute Christians.

When all the terrible woes have taken place, we are told that God will bring everyone to final judgement. The harlot city (Babylon is here an appropriate symbol for Rome) will be destroyed for her oppression of the peoples of the earth (chapters 17-20). Finally, the New Age will dawn in which a new city, will replace the fallen harlot (chapters 21-22). A new heaven and a new earth will appear in which God will be with his people:

> "He will dwell with them, and they shall be his people...
> and he will wipe away every tear from their eyes, and
> death shall be no more..." (21:5)

This is to be the heritage of the "one who overcomes" and remains faithful to the end.

The permanent value of the Revelation to John has often been obscured by the speculation it has occasioned about some far-distant time when the world stops. It is in fact a ringing declaration of faith in the ultimate triumph of God over the militant forces of oppression and evil in the world. In the face of the ruthless demand to place the interests of the Empire above the call of God, John urges his fellow-Christians to stand fast to the end. It is a declaration of the liberty of the sons of God that has stirred the hearts of countless Christians caught in the apparently endless struggle for justice and freedom in the world. It is the announcement of a new earth, a new city, a holy city that is to be founded on the triumph of God's will.

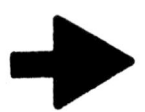

➡ *The book of Revelation may prove difficult to read without a commentary to help you sort out the cryptic symbolism. A good one to use with this or any other New Testament book is:*

INTERPRETER'S ONE-VOLUME COMMENTARY ON THE BIBLE
(Edited by Charles M. Laymon), Abingdon Press, 1971

Also of some help may be the following outline of the book suggested by John C. Gager KINGDOM AND COMMUNITY, THE SOCIAL WORLD OF EARLY CHRISTIANITY. 1975 .

THE STRUCTURE OF REVELATION

VICTORY/HOPE		JUDGEMENT/DESPAIR	
4:1-5:14	Vision of God and the lamb		
		6:1-7	First 6 seals
7:1-8:4	Glory of the faithful 7th seal		
		8:5-9:21	First 6 trumpets
10:1-11	No more delay		
		11:1-14	Attack on the witnesses
11:15-19	7th trumpet		
		12:1-13:18	The dragon and the beast
14:1-7	The Lamb and his hosts		
		14:8-15:1	Harvest of the earth/final wrath
15:2-8	Song of those who overcome		
		16:1-18:24	7 bowls of wrath/ fall of Babylon
19:1-10	Triumph in heaven		
		19:11-20:15	Final judgement
21:1-22:5	The new heaven, the new earth/the holy city		

→ READ: REVELATION

Since the book of Revelation contains a great deal of repetition, you may not wish to read it all in detail right now. To catch the gist of the book however, we suggest reading at least the following:

```
Letters to the seven churches      1:1-3:22
Opening of the seven seals         5:1-8:5
Coming of the beast               13:1-18
Fall of Babylon the Harlot        18:1-24
The new heaven and the new earth  21:1-22:5
```

The contemporary relevance of Revelation comes clear when it is seen as a declaration of hope to oppressed peoples. One could easily despair over the triumph of insanity in this mad world of ours, and indeed, the writer of Revelation sees the dramatic intervention of God as the only hope to avoid it. Apart from God, he sees the world in the process of self-destruction.

1. To whom do you see the message of Revelation addressed today? Move beyond its obvious value to all Christians, and ask yourselves about particular groups of oppressed Christians to whom this word could be spoken now. Make a list of possible audiences.

2. Let each person in your group pick one of the groups on your list above, preferably one they know a little about, as a group of Christians to whom they might write a letter of encouragement. Take ten minutes or so to allow each person to jot down a few notes on what their letter would say.

3. Now go around your group and share the notes you have written. As you do so, note similarities and differences between your attitudes and those of Revelation. Give special attention to the fact that the writer of Revelation assumed the immediacy of Christ's return. If you make the same assumption, how does that affect what you write? If not, what hope do you offer?

From the exercise above, you might ask yourselves about the use of Revelation in the Church today. What is its permanent value to you?

CHAPTER 12

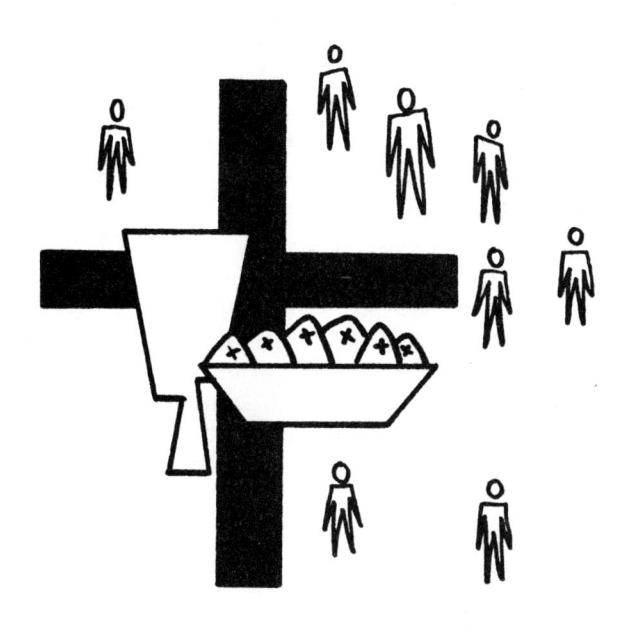

THE UNIVERSAL GOSPEL

"In the fourth century, Jerome chose an eagle as the symbol for the fourth Gospel. He chose well, for this is a soaring, majestic book."
                                        E. W. Bauman

* *

IN THIS CHAPTER WE WILL LOOK AT.....

I. The Universal Gospel
    A. The Johannine literature
    B. The letters of John
    C. The Gospel According to John

II. The Gospel, According to John

I. The Universal Gospel

Our attempt to survey the literature and story of the New Testament has brought us through the turbulent years of the Church's infancy, and up to the point of its establishment as an institution. Its struggles along the way with the issues of Christian belief and identity are reflected in all the writings we have considered to date. By late in the first century and early into the second, the Church had become a predominantly Gentile movement that was beginning to establish a universal vision of God's kingdom. It increasingly saw the Gospel as addressed to the entire *oikoumene* (inhabited world).

In telling the story we have considered all of the major New Testament writings except the so-called Johannine books, that is, the books traditionally attributed to the Apostle John. This group includes the Gospel According to John, and the three letters called I, II and III John.* Though these books were not the last written (that honor probably belongs to II Peter), we are considering them as a fitting end to the New Testament story because they represent the climax of the Church's attempt to address the Gospel to the world. They are surely among the treasures of New Testament writing.

A. The Johannine Literature

As early as the third century a scholarly Bishop of Alexandria named Dionysius saw the close relation in style, language and thought between the Gospel of John and the first letter of John. He also pointed out how greatly the book of Revelation differs from these other two in all the same respects. Though the letters we call II and III John were slow in being recognized as canonical by the Church, they too show a remarkable similarity to the Gospel and the first letter. Together these writings form a third major block of the New Testament along with the works of Paul and Luke. If not from a single author (they are sometimes ascribed to a school), they are certainly at a single pole of New Testament thought and faith.

The tradition ascribing the authorship of the Johannine books to John, the son of Zebedee, dates back to the late second century, and was not seriously questioned until the rise of modern scholarship in the nineteenth century. The objections to such an ascription are substantial, however, and can be summarized as follows:

Traditionally Revelation has been grouped in the corpus of literature attributed to the Apostle John, and thus considered "Johannine". It has at best only a tenuous relation to the other Johannine writings, however, and we have consequently chosen to group it with the other New Testament reactions to persecution.

1. None of these books makes the claim to have been written by the Apostle John, nor is Johannine authorship mentioned in the early Church until about A.D. 180.
2. Neither the Gospel nor the letters show an interest in the details of the life of Jesus such as an immediate disciple might have had.
3. The content of the Johannine writings appears related to the end of the first or beginning of the second century, specifically the struggle against Gnosticism.
4. Clement of Alexandria (A.D. 200) reports that the Gospel of John was written after the Synoptics. This implies a date of A.D. 95-110.
5. While some traditional evidence suggests the Apostle John lived to a ripe old age in Ephesus, Christian writers of the early second century mention only Paul in connection with that Church. There is some evidence to suggest that John died early as a martyr.

Given the uncertainty of the tradition, together with the scarcity of solid evidence either way, it is perhaps best to view the writings of John as from the hand of a great, yet anonymous, Christian who wrote late in the first century, probably from Ephesus or another of the great cities of the eastern Mediterranean area. The significance of this judgement will be clearer as we look more closely at each of the books.

B. The Letters of John

Throughout our study we have frequently come up against the threat Gnosticism represented to the Church. Perhaps you will remember that the Gnostics viewed the physical world as inherently evil and the body as a prison for the soul. They believed all of life to be a struggle between the great cosmic forces of earthly darkness and heavenly light. Salvation was thus dependent upon having a secret, esoteric knowledge, given to the enlightened ones by the light-bringer or redeemer, by which those seeking salvation could escape the material world. Moreover, they believed that Jesus did not have a real physical body, but only *seemed* to have a physical body.

II John is a short note written by the "Elder" (Would the Apostle John have called himself this?) to the "elect lady and her children" (II John 1:1). This latter is probably a reference to a congregation and its members who are warned by the Elder to hold fast the true doctrine of Christ. He closes with greetings from a sister church, and expresses the hope to make a personal visit soon.

III John is addressed by the Elder to a "beloved Gaius". Gaius, evidently a man of some means, is commended for taking in travelling missionaries, and warned of impending trouble in the church from a man named Diotrephes. The letter implies that Gaius is a member of the same congregation to which II John had been written, and that Diotrephes is spreading Gnostic teachings while arrogantly seeking to establish his own authority in the congregation. The Elder makes it clear that he will deal personally with Diotrephes as soon as he arrives.

> READ:
> II, III JOHN
>
> *II and III John are brief and can be read quickly. While neither contains substantial theological reflection or insight, they do provide a fascinating glimpse into the life of the early congregations.*

The first letter of John has been treasured by the Church throughout its history. Since the letter moves forward in a kind of spiral chain of thought, it is difficult to put into a simple outline. A better way to understand its message is to recognize the constantly recurring themes around which the author weaves his letter:

MAJOR THEMES OF I JOHN

1. The true faith is the one revealed by God in Jesus.

    Contrary to Gnostic claims, there is not a new or higher revelation, but only "that which was from the beginning" (1:1). The love of God revealed in Jesus is constantly reaffirmed in the present experience of the believer (Cf. I John 4:9 and 5:9).

2. To know God is to obey his commandments.

    True faith has ethical implications. To dwell in God is to follow the example of Christ, and to obey his commands (2:7-12). Contrary to Gnostic claims, the human life of Jesus has set the example, and whoever does not do right is "not of God" (3:10).

3. To love God is to love others.

    In opposition to the exclusiveness of the Gnostics, I John testifies that, "If anyone says, 'I love God,' and hates his brother, he is a liar" (4:20). The classic statement, "God is love" (4:8), implies an inclusive love of neighbor that makes no claim to superiority or exclusive fellowship.

> READ:
> I JOHN
>
> *I John should be read thoughtfully and slowly. Take careful note of the characteristic phrases that repeat throughout the book. The same style and language will be encountered in the Gospel of John, which also must be viewed against the background of the Gnostic threat.*

TIME OUT!   A NOTE TO CAREFUL NEW TESTAMENT READERS!

Up to this point we have not commented in detail about the transmission of the New Testament text through the centuries. A brief note is in order here, however, because we have in front of us an example of the difficulties that have arisen as manuscripts were hand copied through the years. Compare the following texts:

King James Version	Revised Standard Version
I John 5:6b-8	I John 5:7-8
And it is the Spirit that beareth witness because the Spirit is truth. **For there are three that bear record in heaven, the Father, the Word, and the Holy Ghost: and these three are one.** And there are three that bear witness in earth, the Spirit, and the water, and the blood, and these three agree in one.	And the Spirit is the witness because the Spirit is the truth. There are three witnesses, the Spirit, the water, and the blood; and these three agree.

Not a single ancient Greek manuscript contains the extra verse in the King James Version. Only a few later Latin versions include it, and it is almost certainly a spurious later addition. It seems likely that the reference to the "three witnesses" prompted a fourth century scribe to add his own trinitarian comment. The water and blood are probably references to Jesus' baptism and crucifixion and imply that these historical events (contrary to Gnostic claims) must be added to the testimony of the Spirit in bearing witness to the truth of Jesus.

TRY THIS

The comment in I John that loving God and loving one's neighbor are inseparable, rings true to what we know of Jesus from the Synoptics and other New Testament writings. It also represents one of the New Testament's classic criteria for "testing the spirits to see whether they are of God" (I John 4:1).

1. The passage in I John 4:7-12 stands in clear opposition to the arrogant and exclusive claims of the Gnostics to superiority in a fellowship of the enlightened. When you are sure that everyone

> in your group understands this Gnostic attitude, allow time for individuals to silently re-read the passage cited above.
>
> 2. While many Gnostic elements may be present in Christianity yet today, it is likely that contemporary Christians will read I John 4:7-12 against a very different background. Make a list on a blackboard or large piece of paper of potential situations which might make this passage relevent to our own day. Ask yourselves:
>
>   - Where does the Gnostic-like attitude of exclusiveness exist in the Church in our own time?
>   - Who within the larger ecumenical Church scene is inclined to look down on whom? Who are today's 'true believers'? Or today's second-class Christians?
>
> 3. When a short list has been developed, ask one person in your group to re-read the passage in I John 4:7-12, substituting names or groups from your list for John's terms "one another", "brother", and other pronouns.
>
> 4. With this exercise as background, discuss how you might appropriate the meaning of this passage for the Church now.

C. The Gospel According to John

The study of the Johannine literature brings to a close our survey of the New Testament. The Gospel of John, though not the last among New Testament writings, provides a fitting conclusion to this story because it probably represents the Church's most profound attempt to understand the meaning of Jesus. It is a Gospel of many unique qualities that has always appealed to the seasoned scholar and the beginning student alike. Virtually every phrase in it bears a simple, direct meaning, and yet simultaneously leads the reader into the awesome depths of the mystery of God in the world.

If, when you passed from Mark to Matthew and then to Luke, you were impressed by the similarity among the Synoptics, your chief reaction when you read the Gospel According to John will almost certainly be one of amazement at its difference from the other three. Not only is the content quite different, but so also is the language, the style, and the portrait of Jesus. So striking are these differences that almost any accounting of John's Gospel must begin by addressing the issue of its relation to the Synoptics.

JOHN AND THE SYNOPTICS

Perhaps you will remember that in the Synoptics the career of Jesus is located largely in Galilee. He comes to Jerusalem only for the great Passover celebration during which he is crucified. In John, however, Jesus is in Jerusalem on several occasions, and one thus gains the impression of a much longer public ministry than is described by the other three Gospels.

In John many incidents occur that are not recorded in the Synoptics at all: the wedding at Cana (2:1-11); the story of Nicodemus (3:1-21); the dialogue with the Samaritan woman (4:7-42); the healing at the pool of Bethzatha (5:1-9); the healing of the man born blind (9:1-12); the raising of Lazarus (11:1-44); and the washing of the disciples' feet (13:1-20). Conversely, there are many incidents in the Synoptics that have no parallel in John: the birth narratives, the baptism of Jesus, his temptation, the transfiguration, and the agony in Gethsemane. John also omits any story of the Last Supper in the upper room. The temple-cleansing incident which occurs in Jesus' last week in all the Synoptics, is placed near the beginning of Jesus' ministry by John. Most puzzling of all, John places Jesus' last meal with his disciples on the day *before* Passover, whereas the Synoptics all imply it was the Passover meal itself.

Out of such a list of differences it is not surprising that the portrait of Jesus painted by the Gospel of John is also different than that of the Synoptics. John includes no parables, few short sayings, no exorcisms, and pictures Jesus as openly conscious of his messianic mission. There is no messianic secret as in Mark, nor any interest in historical items as in Luke. While there is much teaching of Jesus in both Matthew and John, the style and language are radically different. You might take the time to re-read Matthew 5-7 (the Sermon on the Mount) and then compare it with John 13-15. The differences will be obvious. John replaces the pithy statements and colorful parables of the Synoptics with long discourses on recurring themes, all cast in stylized patterns that John uses to probe the inner meaning and consciousness of Jesus.

All of this discussion about similarities and differences between John and the Synoptics obviously raises questions about John's sources. Did he know the Synoptics? Did he have independent traditions to draw on? If so, what can we learn about them that will help us see John in relation to the early Church? Satisfactory answers to these questions are hard to come by, and nothing like a consensus exists among scholars on these issues, but most are inclined to believe that John did know Mark, possibly also Luke, and that he also had access to a tradition about Jesus' miracles that the Synoptic writers did not know.

What may be even more important, however, is what John has done with the traditional material he did have available. Give careful attention to the parallel below because it provides a typical example of John's reflective re-working of the tradition:

JOHN 12:25-26	MARK 8:34-35
He who loves his life loses it, and he who <u>hates his life in this world</u> will keep it for <u>eternal life</u>. If anyone serves me he must follow me; and <u>where I am, there shall my servant be also</u>; if anyone serves me, <u>the Father will honor him</u>.	If any man would come after me, let him deny himself, and take up his cross and follow me. For whoever would save his life will lose it; and whoever loses his life for my sake and the Gospel's will save it.

Note carefully the highlighted phrases in the passage from John. They are typical emphases in John's Gospel, and characteristic of the way John uses the events in Jesus' life to comment theologically upon recurrent themes. While the Synoptics include a great deal of such theological interpretation, it is usually implicit and restrained. In John it is explicit and abundant. As we get into the heart of the Gospel we shall look more closely at some of these themes John has interjected into the Markan passage above.

AUTHOR, DATE, PURPOSE

Earlier in this chapter we commented upon the problem of identifying the author of the Johannine writings. That need not be repeated here except to remind ourselves that like the Letters, the Gospel of John is probably the work of an anonymous Christian writing late in the first century or early in the second. It is impossible to say more than this because our sources are too scanty. Fortunately, it makes little difference that we know this author's name; what is impressive is his witness to Jesus as the Christ.

The earliest use of John's Gospel we know about was in Egypt in the late second century. Most scholars, however, are inclined to believe the Gospel originated in either Syria or Palestine. The recently discovered Dead Sea Scrolls have made it clear that Gnostic and Hellenistic influence were widespread in Palestine in the first century, so that for the first time the Johannine concern with these philosophies no longer seems out of place against a Jewish background.

It is the theologizing tendency of John, its anti-Gnostic viewpoint, and its use of Hellenistic language and symbols that have inclined most interpreters to date the book near the turn of the first century. By that time Synagogue Judaism (the temple had been destroyed in A.D. 70) was in open conflict with the Christian movement, a circumstance which John seems to fit well. In John the enemies of Jesus become simply "the Jews", rather than specific parties within Judaism as in the earlier situation of the Synoptics. Probably the best we can say is that John seems to represent the culmination of the Church's attempts to understand Jesus over against the turbulent religious world of the late first century that included Hellenistic Judaism, Greek Philosophy, Gnosticism, and the growing antipathy between Christians, Jews and the Roman world.

Our lack of knowledge of the circumstances under which John was written does not prevent a clear understanding of the author's purpose. John tells us plainly why he writes:

> "Now Jesus did many other things in the presence of his disciples which are not written in this book; but these are written that you might believe that Jesus is the Christ, the Son of God, and that believing you might have (eternal) life in his name." (20:31)

With magnificent simplicity this statment sums up the whole thrust of John's effort. Look more closely at what it involves. John tells us that Jesus:

> "did many other signs..."

That is, our author's primary interest is not to add to the historical fund of knowledge about Jesus. What incidents he has chosen to include are used to point beyond themselves to the theological meaning of what was going on, namely:

> "that Jesus is the Christ, the Son of God..."

From the majestic prologue of the book (1:1-18), right on through to the story of the crucifixion and resurrection, John presents Jesus as the one who reveals the glory of the Father who has been at work since the beginning of time working out the redemption of the world. To John, Jesus is the living embodiment of God's expression of himself, and it is to this that the "signs" point which John has chosen to include.

Finally, John concludes:

> "...and that believing, you might have (eternal) life through his name."

Here is the crux of the matter. John has written in order to elicit belief, and through that, to hold out the offer of eternal life in Jesus' name.

The theme of "eternal life" is an important one throughout John's Gospel. It is the author's terminology for what the Synoptics call the "kingdom of God". Nowadays we are easily misled by the term "eternal" into thinking that John is talking about a far distant reality after death, but throughout the Gospel, John places his emphasis on the *present* reality of this new life. The one who hears and believes has *already* "passed from death to life" (5:24). To be sure, John conceives this new life as transcending time and place, but it is primarily the quality of this new life of the believer that John proclaims in Jesus' name.

You may remember from our earlier discussions of the return of Christ the trauma its delay caused in the Church. Both Paul and other New Testament writers repeatedly affirmed their faith in the full completion of what Christ had begun in the face of waning hope and increasing discouragement in the Church. In John's Gospel the outlook is quite different. It expresses what Biblical scholars call *realized* eschatology. That is, John views the fulfillment as having *already* come in the life of the believer. Instead of a distant hope in the future, John asserts that the glory of God has already begun to blossom in the lives of those who believe in Jesus' name. It is not in the future, but in the present reality of the new life that Jesus reveals God's glory. Thus we have in capsule form the whole thrust of John's message summarized for us in the Gospel itself:

"These things are written that you might believe..."

Before we attempt to look further at specific passages in John, it will be helpful to get an overview of the Gospel's structure. Its outline is rather simple and straight forward:

```
              THE STRUCTURE OF JOHN
    I.   The Prologue:
         A.  God, the Word, and the World    1:1-18
         B.  Testimony and preparation       1:19-51
    II.  The Book of Signs                   2:1-12:50
    III. Jesus and the Twelve                13:1-17:26
    IV.  Death and Resurrection              18:1-20:31
    V.   Appendix (A later addition)         21:1-25
```

Before we comment further upon the message of John, we might take note of several textual difficulties. Virtually unanimous opinion exists that chapter 21 is a later addition to the Gospel. It follows the natural ending of the book (20:30-31) with additional resurrection appearances in Galilee. Another probable addition to the original text is the story of the woman caught in adultery (7:53-8:11). Though most commentators agree that the story is likely an authentic memory of Jesus, none of our earliest manuscripts of John include it.

THE MESSAGE OF JOHN

While we cannot comment at length on many important passages in John without confusing our overview purpose, we have chosen to do so on three typically Johannine texts: the prologue in 1:1-18; the story of Nicodemus in 3:1-21; and Jesus' prayer for his disciples in chapter 17. You may want to read each of these passages prior to our comment about them.

PROLOGUE: READ JOHN 1:1-18

The prologue to John has rightly been considered among the gems of the New Testament. It was possibly an early Christian hymn which John used to introduce the glory of God revealed by Jesus who "became flesh and dwelt among us." Into the middle of the hymn John has interjected his own comments about John the Baptist (vss. 6-8 and 15) in order to make clear that it is Jesus, and not John, who is the Christ. (Is this a veiled polemic against the followers of John the Baptist?) At the end of the prologue (vss. 17-18) John gives us his own summary statement which, like that in 20:30-31, can easily stand as a capsule of the entire Gospel.

Two things in the hymn require careful comment. First, there is the identity of the "word". Christian readers easily assume that the author intends us to understand he is talking about Jesus, and indeed, in verse 17 he names Jesus as his subject. But in the hymn itself, John is dealing with a concept that encompasses more than simply the man Jesus of Nazareth. The term "word" (*logos* in Greek) was a familiar one in Greek philosophy which was used to suggest the notion of divine reason, principle, or utterance. Earlier commentators were inclined to see this Greek idea of cosmic rationality in the background of John's use of the term. In recent years, however, there has grown a new appreciation that the background may not be Greek at all, but rather the Old Testament idea of the creating word of God spoken of in Genesis 1. Both Genesis and John begin with the phrase, "In the beginning...", and thus the parallel may be intentional on John's part.

This leads us to the second comment we ought to make, namely, that John's application of this Logos concept to Jesus is clearly anti-gnostic: "The word became flesh..." What is implied is not so much that the *man* Jesus participated with God in creation, but that everything God was doing in creation has become incarnate in Jesus who now himself reveals the fulness of God's glory. Contrary to Gnostic ideas of a purely spiritual revelation of God in the world, and a purely spiritual Jesus as his Son, John reaffirms the material reality of all that God has done, together with the physical incarnation of that in Jesus his Son.

THE STORY OF NICODEMUS

The story of Nicodemus comes in the middle of what we have called the "book of signs". This book consists of seven miracles of Jesus, each of which provides the occasion for extended theological commentary in the form of dialogues and speeches of Jesus. Many scholars have noticed that John has a characteristic pattern of narration that begins with

>AN EVENT...
>>and then moves to
>
>>A DIALOGUE...
>>>between Jesus and the other
>>>characters; ending with
>>
>>>A MONOLOGUE...
>>>>in which Jesus gives his own
>>>>theological statement of the matter.

Events thus become the platform off which theological interpretation is given, much as the Church today uses the historical Jesus as the basis for theologizing in its own time and place.

You may want to look briefly at each of the seven miracle stories that make up John's book of signs. Here are the seven:

1.	Changing water to wine at Cana	2:1-11
2.	Curing the official's son	4:46-54
3.	Curing the paralytic at Bethzatha	5:1-15
4.	Miraculous feeding in Galilee	6:1-15
5.	Walking on water	6:16-21
6.	Healing a blind man in Jerusalem	9:1-41
7.	Raising of Lazarus	11:1-54

You may want to mark these in the margin of your Bible for further reference.

READ: JOHN 3:1-21

Typical of these incidents John uses to present dialogues and speeches of Jesus is the story of Nicodemus in Chapter 3. Nicodemus, a "ruler of the Jews", comes to Jesus by night to inquire about Jesus' meaning. (Such nighttime inquiry was good rabbinic practice.) Nicodemus is impressed by the signs (!) Jesus performs, and concludes he must be a teacher sent from God. Jesus' reply seemingly has nothing to do with Nicodemus' inquiry, but introduces the notion of being "born anew". Nicodemus is confused. He wonders how a man can enter the womb and be reborn since the term Jesus has just used can carry that connotation. Jesus replies by explaining his earlier ambiguous comment with the statement, "Unless one is born of water (baptism) and the Spirit, he cannot enter the kingdom of God". Again Nicodemus is perplexed, "How can this be?" Whereupon Jesus launches into a monologue explaining that whoever believes "may have eternal life" (vs.15).

The pattern is typical of Jesus' dialogues and speeches in John's Gospel. Events become the occasion for dialogue, misunderstanding, and eventual clarification by Jesus. The tendency of Nicodemus (and all who heard the Gospel story) to misunderstand the meaning of the signs requires careful exposition from the lips of Jesus himself. It is thus the earthly Jesus who explains the meaning of the events, not the other way around.

JESUS' PRAYER FOR HIS DISCIPLES

READ: JOHN 17

This well-known passage deserves far more detailed comment than we can give it here, but its importance is such that we cannot pass over it completely. The chapter consists of an extended prayer of Jesus offered on behalf of his disciples. (In the latter half of the Gospel it is the disciples who are Jesus' prime concern.) Having spoken at length with the disciples of his impending departure from them, and of their struggle in the world which will be increasingly hostile toward them, Jesus lifts his eyes to heaven and prays.

As always, the concern is with eternal life. "And this is eternal life, that they know thee the only true God, and Jesus Christ (Would Jesus have referred to himself this way?) whom thou hast sent" (17:3). Jesus is concerned that his followers overcome the world, and speaks in language that sounds very much like what we might expect in behalf of Christians caught in the struggles of the late first century.

Jesus does not pray that his disciples be taken out of the world. He declares no gnostic promise of escaping this vale of tears to an other-worldly existence elsewhere. Rather, he prays that they should be kept safe in the world. The concluding note is one of unity between Jesus and his disciples who, like Jesus himself, are to display the love of God which reveals his glory in the world.

> *It is important, of course, to remember that the term "world" used here does not mean the physical creation. It rather refers to the world humankind creates in alienation from God. It is the opposite of eternal life. To assume, as many do, that John is speaking of the material creation would lead to the Gnostic devaluation of all things physical - a notion John specifically refutes with the statement that Jesus came in the flesh.*

II. The Gospel, According to John

The concluding sections of John's Gospel tell the story of Jesus' death and resurrection. John's passion story shows remarkable similarity to that in Mark, though John's theological flair moves beyond the stark simplicity of Mark's account.

We have already noted that while the Synoptics view the Last Supper as a Passover meal, John reports it having taken place on the Day of Preparation (that is, the day *before* Passover). This means that in John's story Jesus dies on the cross at the very moment the Jewish families are killing the lambs to be used in the Passover meal. Thereby John highlights the testimony of John the Baptist:

"Behold the Lamb of God who takes away the sin of the world." (1:29)

This has been Jesus' mission from the beginning. The final glory of the resurrected Christ seals all that Jesus means as the Son of God who is the occasion for God's redemption of the world. Thus it is *after* the resurrection that Jesus also gives his final instructions to the Church:

"As the Father has sent me, even so I send you." (20:21)

In many ways this Gospel According to John represents the culmination of New Testament thought. As we have seen, Christianity was born amidst the enthusiastic expectation of Jesus' imminent return, and the final establishment of God's kingdom. At first there was little thought for ecclesiastical organization or any of the other things that implied extended life in the present order of things. The theological insights and ethical exhortations of Paul had been written for a generation that anticipated the in-breaking of the New Age at any moment, and were thus never fully developed for the generations that followed. As time wore on, the Synoptic Gospels were composed because the Church felt the need to ground its life in the experience of Jesus. Other authors began to spell out the implications of the Gospel for the emerging institution's life in the world. The author of Ephesians prepared a compendium of Paul's theology geared for his own day, while other Christian leaders reacted to the growing persecution of the Church with a call to courage and faith.

It fell to the writer of the Gospel According to John, however, to compose the culminating statement of the Church's faith at a time when the hope for Christ's immediate return had faded and it had become evident that the Church would have to remain in, if not of, the world. It is significant that such a theological statement comes to us in the form of a Gospel - a story of the Good News of Jesus - and that this Gospel should have as its overarching purpose the elicitation of belief in the hearts of those who read it. It seems significant that the issues of the Church's ongoing life in the world should be confronted most profoundly in the life of Jesus. That is John's abiding message to all who seek eternal life.

READ: JOHN

Now is the time to read the Gospel According to John. While it can be read substantially as it appears in most English texts, you may want to reverse the order of chapters 5 and 6 in order to avoid the confusion of Jesus' movement. Also note that in most translations 7:53-8:11 is appended in a footnote in recognition that it is not included in our earliest texts.

TRY THIS

More than any other New Testament document, the Gospel According to John emphasizes the present reality of the Christian hope. While John's concept of "eternal life" obviously transcends time, it is nonetheless described as the *present* reality for those who believe.

1. Put the term "eternal life" on the blackboard or a large piece of paper at the front of the room. Ask class participants to play a word association game with the term by listing on their own worksheet as many word associations as they can muster in three or four minutes.

2. Break your group up into pairs or triads and ask participants to share with each other the associations they have drawn. Allow time for people to listen to the 'flavor' of what comes through on each person's list.

3. Bring your group back together again and share insights, giving special attention to anything *new* participants may have learned about the term either from their own reading or from the word associations of others. How does this compare with the traditional notion of eternal life as merely denoting the length of time Christians will live after death? You might also ask how many of the ideas shared have to do with the present moment as over against a distant future.

If out of this exercise emerges a sense of the liberating, freeing truth of God which radically alters the *quality* of life, you will have caught a taste of the vision of John.

Appendix I

Where do we go from here in New Testament Study?

Throughout our discussion of the New Testament, we have constantly tried to bring the larger picture into focus. Many details have been deliberately left aside so as not to confuse our overview objective. Our hope has been that after completing this study the reader would be able to stand back and view the sweep of the New Testament as it emerged out of the life of the early Church.

If that objective has to any degree been accomplished, it should now be easier for the reader to go back for a deeper look at any particular New Testament passage or book with some understanding of its relation to the whole. It should be easier to set things in their proper historical or literary context, and thus gain a richer understanding of what a given New Testament author was trying to say. Above all, it ought to have provided some background from which to launch out on your own into new ventures in New Testament study.

To much of the Christian Church today the Bible is a closed book, not because of a lack of interest in its message, but because of inadequate tools with which to study. The gulf of two thousand years is a difficult one for many people to cross, even with the help of modern translations. Our study has thus attempted to provide the reader with a few tools for serious Bible study. The historical/critical approach to the New Testament assumes that the actual setting and circumstances that produced the documents are important keys to their understanding. It also assumes that some measure of historical homework is necessary today to bridge the gulf of two millenia. Strange names, places, ideas, and beliefs are much easier to deal with when seen operating in the life-situation of real people. Moreover, when such an approach is taken to the New Testament writings, it should be obvious to almost anyone that there is more here than meets the casual eye. A greatly enriched understanding is one of the rewards of this kind of study.

A key question, however, is where to go from here? Gaining an overview is not an end in itself, but rather a prelude to deeper study. The same historical/critical tools used to develop this overview can be applied with even greater benefit to particular passages and books. It is hoped that completion of this study will give you confidence to tackle the New Testament in a variety of additional ways:

1. STUDY A NEW TESTAMENT BOOK

    Individual New Testament books can be studied either in great detail or as an overview project. More detail on the historical/critical background of the writings is available in any good Bible dictionary, and helpful information on particular passages can be found in many commentaries. Immersing yourself in a particular book for a period of time could be a good next step after the study you have done here.

2. STUDY A NEW TESTAMENT AUTHOR

Study of a single New Testament author with a view to gaining an understanding of his particular viewpoint is another rewarding kind of study. You might take Paul, Luke, or John and live with their writings until you gain a sense or feel for who they were and how they thought. Such study is especially enriching when a second author is studied who can then be viewed comparatively with the one studied first.

3. STUDY A NEW TESTAMENT FIGURE

The most obvious figure in the New Testament appropriate for further study is Jesus himself, but the horizon need not stop there. One can also string together bits and pieces on a few of the disciples, on Titus, Timothy, John Mark, or a host of other New Testament figures. You might also try comparing Paul's comments about himself with those made about him in Acts.

4. STUDY A NEW TESTAMENT THEME

Gaining an overview of the New Testament writings should be especially helpful background for tackling particular New Testament themes. There are the obvious ones such as *faith,* or *salvation,* or *the kingdom of God,* but equally possible are such topics as: the Church's response to heresy, the role and place of women in the Church, the respective writer's views of Jesus, their expectations for the future, etc.

5. STUDY A NEW TESTAMENT PASSAGE

Individual passages or pericopes can always be studied with great benefit. Your study here, together with heavy use of Bible dictionaries and commentaries, should enable you to draw out the significance of most New Testament passages in a way that will enable you to say what they mean to you personally. That, after all, is the point of it all.

Appendix II

A Summary of New Testament Writings

BOOK	AUTHOR	A.D. DATE	THEME OR PURPOSE
Matthew	uncertain	80-100	Written to show Jesus to be the promised Messiah. Stresses discipleship, and may have been a manual for new Christians.
Mark	Mark	70	Bold statement of the Good News that the suffering Jesus is the Christ.
Luke	Luke	80-90	Occasioned by the need for a clear account of the story of Christ: "That you may know the truth concerning the things of which you have been informed."
John	uncertain "John"?	90-110	Written that "...you might believe that Jesus is the Christ, the Son of God, and that believing you might have life through his name."
Acts	Luke	80-90	Originally a sequel to Luke. Written to give an orderly account of the early Christian missionary effort by which the Gospel spread into the Gentile world.
Romans	Paul	56-57	Outlines Paul's understanding of the Christian faith, written to prepare the Church in Rome for Paul's intended visit. One of the most profound theological works in the New Testament.
I Corinthians	Paul	55-56	Paul's teaching and advice on problems that had arisen in the Corinthian congregation. Practical Christianity. Probably

Book	Author	Date	Description
			the second in a series of at least four letters.
II Corinthians	Paul	55-56	Similar to above. Includes a great deal of Paul's attitude toward his own ministry. A compilation of fragments from two, possibly three letters.
Galatians	Paul	54	Paul defends the freedom of the Christian against those trying to impose a legalistic view of our relationship to God.
Ephesians	uncertain	90?	A general letter meant to be circulated amongst the churches. Written to strengthen the faith of the readers. Stresses the unity of the Church.
Philippians	Paul	58-63	Reminiscences and reflections from prison in Rome. Thanks the Philippian congregation for its concern.
Colossians	uncertain, but Paul likely	58-63	Written to warn against growing distortions of the faith, especially in regard to the meaning and place of Christ.
I and II Thessalonians	Paul	50-51	Emphasis on sober moral life. Has a sense of the nearness of Christ's return and includes Paul's advice to the Thessalonians regarding it.
I Timothy	uncertain, Uses "Paul" as a pseudonym	100-110	Concerned with Church order, organization, doctrine. Instructions for Church leadership are given.
II Timothy	Same as I Timothy	100-110	Similar to I Timothy.
Philemon	Paul	58-63	Onesimus, a runaway slave, became a Christian under Paul's influence. Paul writes to his owner asking him to receive Onesimus back, not as a slave, but as a brother in Christ.

Book	Author	Date	Description
Hebrews	uncertain	95	Written to persecuted Christians to encourage their endurance in the faith, and to remind them of God's supreme revelation of himself in Jesus Christ.
James	uncertain	90-110	Written to the "twelve tribes", probably meaning all Christians. Stresses good works, warns the wealthy, encourages patience. Warns Christians against misconceptions of faith which forget moral conduct.
I Peter	uncertain, possibly Peter	62-63 if Peter A.D. 95 if not	Written to persecuted Christians in Asia Minor to encourage them against false teachers and urge faithful conduct.
II Peter	uncertain	150?	A general letter to Christians urging them to grow in faith. Warns against false teachers. Incorporates Jude in Chapter 2.
I John	"John"?	90-110	Written against false teaching of the Gnostics. Stresses Jesus' humanity. Love of neighbor is seen as the test of love of God.
II John	"John"?	90-110	Warns the "elect lady and her children" (the Church) against false teachers.
III John	"John"?	90-110	Personal letter to a Christian named Gaius. Warns against a false teacher named Diotrophes.
Jude	"Jude"?	110-120?	A diatribe against those who lost sight of the need for high moral conduct.
Revelation	An unknown John, probably not the disciple	95-96	Written to Christians suffering persecution under the Emperor Domitian in Asia Minor. It is a cryptic (therefore heavily symbolic) message asserting that God, not Rome, will be triumphant in the end. Christians are encouraged to be faithful even unto death.

Appendix III

The Ultimate "Try This"!

Perhaps the ultimate "try this" is when the reader puts to use what this study has uncovered in his own work with the New Testament. There is no reason to assume that the New Testament must be mediated to the Church by select experts who purport to give the final interpretation of any passage. The historical/critical scholarship we have been talking about is meant to enrich the Church's study, *not pre-empt it*. Our hope is that you will treat the material in this book as precisely that: enrichment for your own study of the New Testament and not a replacement for it.

1. Pick a New Testament passage that you would like to study further on your own. We shall refrain from making suggestions so as not to pre-empt your own decision about what you want to pursue.

2. When a passage is chosen, review the study material in this book that will help you set the passage in its historical context. Or, if you want more detail, look up the New Testament book in which your passage is found in a Bible dictionary and read the background article. Give particular note to anything that will help you understand the needs of the particular Christian community to whom your passage was written.

3. When you are satisfied that you have a handle on the setting and context of your passage, again use your Bible dictionary to nail down any unfamiliar names, places, events or peculiar words. Give attention to any other Biblical passages cited in the dictionary articles since they may provide additional insight.

4. Particularly noteworthy phrases or concepts can be used as a basis for finding parallel passages with your concordance. How far afield you wish to go in tracking down such references will probably be determined by the scope of your passage and its key ideas.

5. If your passage is in the Synoptics, be sure to search out Synoptic parallels. Give close attention

to differences and similarities in the readings among the various texts. Learn what you can from each author's treatment of the passage.

6. When you are satisfied that you have gathered sufficient material to help you understand what the author was doing, try putting the passage in your own words. A simple summary of it will be a good indication that you have grasped the meaning. Be aware that you may see in the passage what other interpreters have missed, and thus take the occasion to discuss the passage with other Christians. The *shared* insights of the Christian community are what make the Bible a living book in the Church today.

7. Finally, try to put down in a sentence or two what the passage means to you personally in your own time and place. If necessary, transpose its message into the midst of the contemporary issues of faith and practice with which you and your society must wrestle. That, in the final analysis, is the promise and reward of studying the Bible for yourself!

LEADER'S GUIDE
INTO ALL THE WORLD

INTRODUCTION

Studying the New Testament is not an end in itself—as if factual knowledge about it was a worthwhile acquisition for its own sake. The real objective of New Testament study is encounter with the living God. While the necessity of some factual knowledge is inescapable if one seeks to read the New Testament intelligently, the best type of study seeks to integrate information with actual life experience in such a way that one senses the implications of faith for everyday living. Put another way, one does not study Romans so that he will know what Romans has to say, but so that what Romans has to say will change one's life. Learning is change, not answers!

One could easily view the New Testament as a partner in dialogue about one's own life and the life of the world. By viewing New Testament authors, characters, audiences and stories in their original life-situations, it is possible to engage them in a kind of conversation that is dynamic and ongoing. Wrestling back and forth with the issues and concerns of real people who were caught in much the same struggles of hope and despair that affects our lives, is to read in search of growth and understanding rather than mere information. That is New Testament study in the best sense of the term.

A. AN APPROACH TO THE STUDY OF THE NEW TESTAMENT

Since your role as leader will be to facilitate your group's study of life-situations along with the New Testament itself, it will be important for you to recognize a few of the assumptions upon which the study is based.

1. *The new testament is best studied with other Christians.* The New Testament is, after all, the book of the church. Most of it was addressed to congregations to meet the needs they shared together as Christian communities. This is not to denigrate the value or need for individual study. It does emphasize the need to be in dialogue with other Christians as we study so that our individual blindspots can be put into perspective and our individual insights shared.

2. *The study group is at its best when it becomes a community.* A group is not necessarily a community. It becomes so when individuals in the group see themselves as sharing life together in dialogue, concern, and interest in mutual growth. The more emphasis on mutual support and growth, and the less on proving pet doctrinal points, the better the New Testament itself will be able to contribute to the process of learning and growth.

3. *Adults learn in many different ways.* Some adults are readers; some are not. Many are activists who learn by doing; others are more analytical and like to reflect and investigate. Flexible groupings and varied educational approaches are needed to reflect the diversity of adult learning styles.

4. *Learning experiences are better viewed as events or happenings rather than classes in the traditional sense.* The door to varied educational approaches is opened when we get past the closed concept of one person (the teacher) passing information on to other persons (the students). A content-shift, in which information passes from the head of the teacher to the head of the student, is not necessarily learning.

   For example, if it is a skill you are trying to teach, a training lab will be more valuable than a traditional lecture. If personal growth is your objective, a process that allows for group interaction is required. If the end result of your program is supposed to be some kind of action in the community, an action/reflection approach may best suit your needs. For too long we have assumed that the mere transmission of information instituted adequate New Testament study, whereas the New Testament itself assumes that the role of the Gospel is to change one's life.

5. *Inductive learning is natural to most adults.* Inductive learning is learning by discovery. Or, to put it another way, it is learning from experience. It assumes that the role of the leader in adult study groups is more that of facilitator, or enabler, than that of information-transmitter. Inductive learning brings into play not only cognitive faculties but also intuition, sensory perception, emotional awareness, etc. A simple illustration is afforded in the way a person learns a new skill. In the process of doing the task one slowly becomes aware of subtle problems or difficulties and what to do about them. Only then does theorizing about the activity begin to make sense as an explanation of what is going on. So, for example, in the process of reading the four Gospels one will *discover* their very different perceptions of Jesus. Almost any reader will make that discovery entirely on his own, and it is at that moment that the question will arise about why and how this came to be. Then the base is laid for meaningful discussion of the issue of the historical Jesus, whereas discussion of this issue prior to the discovery would seem to many people an unnecessary and irrelevant complication of the study.

   It is for this reason that most of the group exercises (the "TRY THIS" sections) in the *Into All the World* text are inductive in nature. They are aimed at helping people to discover or gain a feel for concepts and issues before they are discussed analytically. It is hoped that group leaders will take such group processes seriously as a means of allowing the New Testament to become a partner in living dialogue within the group.

B. THE LEADER'S PREPARATION

As in any group learning process, the role of the teacher, or facilitator, is a key one. You will have a major role in setting the style of what is done as well as the depth at which it is approached. Because this is so, it is worthwhile thinking through ahead of time exactly what you want to have happen and what strategy is needed to facilitate it. It almost goes without saying that group exercises, audiovisual materials, and other process resources are not intended as an excuse for lack of leader preparation.

1. Be sure to think through ahead of time the list of resources you will need for each group session. In many instances materials need to be gathered in advance for the group exercises, or equipment is needed for tapes, filmstrips, or other audiovisual items.

2. While the explanations given in the group exercises are usually clear and simple, experience indicates that different people read directions in different ways. It will be important, therefore, to think your way through each group exercise you plan to use ahead of time. Try to visualize the process step by step, so that you are sure you know what it is you want your group to do.

3. Tapes and filmstrips available for use with *Into All the World* (see below under Resources) should also be previewed by the leader. Decide how and when you want them used so as to enhance the objectives you are trying to reach. Information as to what is available and how to order it is given on page 2 of this guide.

4. The leader's preparation will obviously include his/her own study of the New Testament ahead of time. Since the *Into All the World* materials are designed to give participants an overview of the New Testament, detailed leader preparation on individual New Testament passages will not usually be required. What is more likely is that discussions will raise questions about particular passages only as illustrations of broader issues being discussed. At this point the leader will have to rely on his/her own fund of background in New Testament study.

   Experienced leaders will have substantial background on which to draw. Others should have ready access to reference works and resources that will enable their group to investigate and find answers for themselves. In the long run, such facilitation of group inquiry may be more valuable than ready answers on the part of the group leader.

5. In section c, #6 of this Leader's Guide is a list of bibliographical resources for the leader's own study. The bibliography is annotated to give you an idea of the technical level of the material as well as its major content. Regardless of the leader's level of technical knowledge, any of the major introductions to the New Testament listed in the bibliography would be helpful with detailed background for the leader's own preparation: for some they would be merely a helpful review, while for others they would repay careful and detailed study.

C. RESOURCES

You will not need many resources, but it is important that they be gathered ahead of time. Some of the things needed can be scrounged from home, others bought at local bookstores, and a few ordered ahead of time by mail. Be sure to review the material you plan to cover in each session and have your resources on hand before the group arrives.

1. Chapter I of *Into All the World* introduces students to a historical/critical study of the Bible. It comments about resources such as Bible dictionaries, concordances, newer translations, etc. It would be a good idea to have all these resources on hand at your first session and go over each with the group to make sure its use is well understood.

2. Elsewhere in *Into All the World* other written resources are cited. A *Gospel Parallels*, for example, is a recommended tool. So also are various commentaries. These too should be available for use in class sessions so that everyone understands their value. It might also be helpful to know where in your community such resources can be purchased so that students wishing to buy their own know where to go.

3. Many of the group exercises call for materials for group activities. Blackboard (or overhead projector), large sheets of paper, marking pens, glue, old magazines and pictures, etc. are called for. The leader should review each exercise and acquire the needed materials or equipment in advance.

4. It would be helpful to have maps of Palestine and the Mediterranean world on the walls and available for use at all times. They will come into frequent play as the New Testament is discussed.

5. A major resource available for use with *Into All the World* is *The New Testament World: Adult Bible Study Resources Kit*, which contains a filmstrip on the geography of the New Testament lands and a series of tape recordings on understanding New Testament concepts. *The New Testament World: Geography of the New Testament Lands* is a filmstrip that provides comment on projected maps of both the Mediterranean world of the early church and Palestine in Jesus' day. It includes a narrated travelogue through these areas to show viewers what the land looks like, how its cities stood, and how its people lived. *The New Testament World: Studies in New Testament Theology* is a series of tape recordings designed to give additional background on New Testament concepts or issues. Each tape segment is approximately 15 minutes long, and most of them involve some participation on the part of the listeners. Instructions are given on the tapes when listeners are asked to make charts, take notes, jot down reactions, etc. It is very important, therefore, that the leader go through the tapes ahead of time to determine the best way to use them in the group.

   The subjects covered on the tapes are: Tape 1/Side A—Filmstrip Narration; Side B-(1) Historical/Critical Study of the Bible, (2) The Old Testament and the New. Tape 2/Side A-(1) Tuning in on the First Century's Wavelength: A Study of Greek and Hebrew Thought, (2) The Original Message: Sermons in Acts; Side B-(1) The Emerging Christian Community, (2) Discipleship. Tape 3/Side A-(1) Who is this Man? (2) What Really Happened: A Study on the Historical Jesus; Side B-(1) Crucifixion, (2) Resurrection. Tape 4/Side A-(1) Parables of the Kingdom, (2) Worship and Sacraments in the Early Church; Side B-(1) The Meaning of Faith, (2) Hope in the New Age.
   This multimedia resources kit (tapes and filmstrip) may be ordered from: Griggs Educational Service, 1731 Barcelona Street, Livermore, California 94550.

6. *Resources for the leader's own study—New Testament introduction, background works, tools*

   *Baly, Denis, *The Geography of the Bible*. New York: Harper and Row, 1974. (An update of a standard work on the geography of the biblical lands as it relates to the biblical story.)
   Feine, P., Behm, J., and Kummel, W. G., *Introduction to the New Testament*. Nashvlle: Abingdon, 1966. (A fairly technical rewrite of an earlier work. Reasonably complete and up-to-date.)
   Finegan, Jack, *The Archaeology of the New Testament: the Life of Jesus and the Beginning of the Early Church*. New Jersey: Princeton University Press, 1969. (The most extensive and readable work on New Testament archaeology.)
   Fuller, R. H., *A Critical Introduction to the New Testament*. London: Duckworth, 1966. (Less technical, but valuable introduction to the critical problems of New Testament study.)
   Grant, Robert M., *A Short History of the Interpretation of the Bible*, rev. ed. New York: MacMillan, 1963. (A short, but comprehensive survey of the methods Christians have used through the centuries to interpret the Bible.)
   The Interpreter's Dictionary of the Bible (5 vols.). Nashville: Abingdon, 1962. (One of the most exhaustive and up-to-date reference works available.)
   Kee, H. C., Young, F. W., and Froelich, K., *Understanding the New Testament*, 3rd ed. Englewood Cliffs, New Jersey: Prentice-Hall, 1973. (An update of a standard introduction aimed at covering the major issues of critical study. Detailed, but not hard to read.)
   Marxsen, Willi, *Introduction to the New Testament: An Approach to its Problems*, (trans, by G. Buswell). Philadelphia: Fortress Press, 1968. (Very similar to the work by Fuller; written by an outstanding German scholar. Emphasizes questions crucial for interpretation.)
   Moule, C.F.D., *The Birth of the New Testament*. New York: Harper and Row, 1962. (An excellent discussion of the church situations and needs which led to the composition of New Testament books and the formation of the canon.)
   Perrin, Norman, *The New Testament, An Introduction*. New York: Harcourt Brace Jovanovich, 1974 (A newer treatment of the methods and background of New Testament study, together with an exegetical survey of each New Testament book.)
   Richardson, Alan, *A Theological Wordbook of the Bible*, London: SCM Press, 1960. (A helpful treatment of key theological terminology in the Bible.)
   Wright, G. E., *Biblical Archaeology*, rev. ed. Philadelphia: Westminster Press, 1962. (One of the most useful, nontechnical descriptions of the archaeological background of the biblical period available in English.)
   *Young, Robert, *Analytical Concordance to the Bible*. New York: Funk and Wagnalls (n.d.). (An invaluable tool that breaks down each English entry into the several Greek or Hebrew words it translates.)

Commentaries

   The Cambridge Bible Commentary. Cambridge: Cambridge University Press, 1965. (An excellent British commentary series based on the New English Bible. Available in paperback.)
   The Interpreter's Bible (12 Vols.). Nashville: Abingdon, 1952–57. (An exhaustive work now somewhat out of date. The exegetical sections and background articles remain an excellent resource.)
   The Laymen's Bible Commentary. Richmond, Virginia: John Knox Press, 1961. (A brief, easily readable commentary in nontechnical language.)
   Peake's Commentary on the Bible, M. Black and H. H. Rowley, eds. New York: Nelson, 1962. (A one-volume commentary, largely the product of British scholarship. Highly readable.)

*A good set of basic tools

D. USING INTO ALL THE WORLD

There are a variety of ways *Into All the World* can be used. The approach you choose will have to take into account not only the material itself, but also the number and length of class sessions available to you. Below are several suggestions.

ONE-AND-A-HALF HOUR SESSIONS
Session 1.
   -Introduce the overview concept together with your expectations for the study. Indicate what your own role will be.
   -Review the use of the tools for New Testament study.
   -Show Part I of the filmstrip on geography (*The New Testament World; Geography of the New Testament Lands*) or, if unavailable, visually introduce maps of the New Testament lands.
   -Introduce the concept of historical/critical study by using "Historical-Critical Study of the Bible" (Tape 1/Side B) or by an inductive exercise of your own devising. What is important is to show by specific example

that historical-critical study makes a difference in how the text is understood.
- Ask participants to read chapter 1 of *Into All the World*, and to note any questions they may want to bring up at the next session.
- For the leader's own study:
  Perrin, N., *The New Testament: An Introduction*. pp. 3-37.
  Krentz, E., *The Historical-Critical method*. Philadelphia: Fortress Press, 1975.

Session 2
- Allow 10–15 minutes for informal discussion of questions raised by last week's study and the reading assignment for this session.
- Do the TRY THIS exercise on page 24 of *Into All the World*. Allow 20–30 minutes. The written statements to be shared with the group need be only a sentence or two long. Try to evoke how people *feel* about the prospects for a "new age."
- If time permits, do the TRY THIS on page 26. It will take about 20 minutes to create the collage and 15 minutes to discuss it afterward.
- Assign the reading of chapter 2 of *Into All the World* and ask participants to note questions for later discussion.
- For the leader's own study:
  Cambridge Bible Commentary (Introductory Volume). pp. 64-144.

Session 3
- Allow 10–15 minutes for informal discussion of questions raised by last week's study and the week's reading assignment.
- Use "Tuning in on the First Century's Wavelength: A Study of Greek and Hebrew Thought" (Tape 2/Side A) with the group. The tape can simply be played while the group listens and follows instructions. Allow 15–20 minutes for discussion afterward. (Be sure you have listened to the tape ahead of time and know what to expect!)
- Remind the group that "The Old Testament and the New" (Tape 1/Side B) is available for further study. Invite anyone interested to work with it at home and report to the group.
- Assign Chapter 3 of *Into All the World* and the book of Acts in the New Testament. Ask participants to note questions for discussion.
- Leader's own study:
  On this and subsequent chapters dealing with particular New Testament books, leaders may want to consult the introductory articles for each New Testament book found in the *Interpreter's Bible Dictionary*. Available commentaries may also be consulted for particular books.

Session 4
- Allow for discussion of questions raised by reading.
- Do the TRY THIS exercise on page 47. Allow 30–45 minutes. As in any role-playing situation, it is crucial that participants understand the role they are playing.
- Invite the individual(s) who listened to "The Old Testament and the New" (Tape 1/Side B) to report to the group.
- If time permits, do the TRY THIS exercise on page 51. Allow 20–25 minutes.
- Invite individual(s) to use and report back on "The Original Message: Sermons in Acts" (Tape 2/Side A). The tape isolates the content of apostolic preaching as remembered by the new congregations of which Acts tells.
- Assign chapter 4 of *Into All the World*, again asking participants to make note of questions raised by reading.

Session 5
- Since the biblical reading for this week was substantial, you may want to use the summary in Appendix II to refresh the group's memory. The discussion of this material may be considerable, especially in regard to the somewhat complex reconstruction of II Corinthians in *Into All the World*. Be sure to allow time to work through people's questions.
- Do the TRY THIS on page 63. Be aware that this discussion could easily focus on the discrepancies between belief and practice and miss the simple point that they are always intertwined. Allow 30 minutes.
- Assign chapter 5 of *Into All the World* and Paul's letter to the Romans. Ask participants to note questions for later discussion.

Session 6
- Take 10–15 minutes for discussion of questions raised by reading.
- Do the TRY THIS on page 71. The critical nature of this subject for understanding Paul makes it worth the 30–40 minutes this exercise takes to do. Most people will readily understand the human struggle for acceptance, but some may have difficulty relating it to the underlying and often ill-defined struggle for acceptance by God. It is on the relation between these two that the discussion is most profitably centered.
- Additional clarification on the subject of faith may be gained by using, "The Meaning of Faith" (Tape 4/Side B). It could be assigned to an individual for a later report or played at the conclusion of this session as a parting "thought to ponder."
- Assign chapter 6 of *Into All the World*. Ask participants to be especially careful in noting questions raised for them by the style of Synoptic study being proposed.
- Invite use of tape recordings used to date by any who missed them or wants to relisten.

Session 7
- Allow discussion on questions raised by reading. Since this type of Synoptic study may be new to many participants, discussion may be substantial. In preparation the leader may want to consult:
  Marxsen, W., *Introduction to the New Testament*. pp. 112-33.
- Do the TRY THIS exercise on page 82, allowing 20–30 minutes.
- Show Part II of the filmstrip on geography (*The New Testament World: Geography of the New Testament Lands*) or, if unavailable, visually introduce maps of Palestine in Jesus' day.
- Assign chapter 7 of *Into All the World* and the Gospel of Mark. Ask participants to note items for discussion.

Session 8
- Do the TRY THIS exercise on page 88. Allow the discussion that follows to move into the consideration of particular Markan passages that may have raised questions in reading. The TRY THIS exercise can evoke substantial feelings pro and con therefore should not be hurried. If it moves into discussion of particular passages from Mark, as much time can obviously be spent as the group desires. Allow at least 30–40 minutes.
- Assign chapter 8 of *Into All the World* and the Gospel According to Matthew. Ask participants to note questions for discussion.

Session 9
- Do the TRY THIS exercise on page 100. It takes only 15 minutes or so and serves to create a climate for the discussion of the teachings of Jesus.
- Allow 10–15 minutes for questions from reading. Individual Matthean passages may be discussed at whatever length the group desires.
- Play and discuss "Parables of the Kingdom" (Tape 4/Side A) or do the TRY THIS exercise on page 105. Allow 20 minutes.
- Assign chapter 9 of *Into All the World* and the Gospel according to Luke. Ask participants to note items for discussion.

Session 10
- Do the TRY THIS on page 112, allowing 30–45 minutes depending on the size of your group. After participants have shared their "double history" with each other, be sure to take time to summarize the concept in relation to Luke. A good way to do this is to review the examples in Luke 2:2 and 3:1-2.
- Allow 10–15 minutes for questions noted in reading.
- Do the TRY THIS exercise on page 116. Be sure everyone understands the term "apology." Allow 30 minutes.
- Invite individual(s) to use "Discipleship" (Tape 2/Side B) for later reports to the group.
- Assign the reading of the Appendix to Synoptic Study, asking participants to note items for discussion.

Three of the tape recordings are particularly appropriate at this point in the study:

Tape 3/Side A	"What Really Happened: A Study of the Historical Jesus.
Tape 3/Side B	"Crucifixion"
Tape 3/Side B	"Resurrection"

These tapes deal with both our historical knowledge about Jesus and the theological significance of the key events in his life. They may be used in several ways:
- Ask individual(s) to review them carefully *before* Session 11 and be prepared to contribute insights gained to a major discussion of the problem of the historical Jesus during the session.
- Play one or more of them *during* Session 11.
- Loan them out *after* Session 11 to individuals who wish to do more detailed study on their own.

Session 11
- Do the TRY THIS on page 120. In preparation for this discussion the leader may want to consult the excellent discussion of this problem in:
  Fuller, R.H., *The New Testament in Current Study.* pp. 25-53
  If any of the tapes relating to this problem are to be played for the whole group, now is the time. If not, any individuals who listened to them ahead of time should be encouraged to contribute to the discussion of the whole group.
- Pick up any unfinished business from your study of the Synoptics. Problem passages should be discussed in light of the Synoptic parallels whenever possible.
- Loan tape recordings to individuals who wish to use them in pursuing the problem of the historical Jesus on their own. Trade around tapes used earlier.
- Assign chapter 10 of *Into All the World* together with the appropriate Bible readings. Ask participants to note items for discussion.

Session 12
- Do the TRY THIS on page 127. Be careful with the distinction drawn between personal and professional qualifications. Allow about 20–25 minutes for the exercise.
- The TRY THIS on page 130 may be one of the more difficult ones, but it is also one of the more important given the prevalence of gnostic ideas yet today. Difficulties can be easily avoided if the leader has thought through the entire exercise ahead of time and has a clear idea how he/she would fill in the chart. Leaders may be helped by consulting the article by R. M. Grant in *The Interpreter's Dictionary of the Bible* or by looking up the listings under "gnosticism" in Norman Perrin's *The New Testament: An Introduction.*
- Invite individual(s) to use "Worship and Sacraments in the Early Church" (Tape 4/Side A) and report back to the group.
- Assign pages 133-37 of *Into All the World* together with I Peter and Hebrews. Ask participants to note items for discussion.

Session 13
- Allow discussion of questions raised by reading and by the general subject of persecution.
- Using a Bible dictionary, do a little research on the particular charges brought against Christians by the Roman world. Share these with your group as background for discussing present-day tensions between the church and the world.
- Invite reports on "Worship and Sacraments in the Early Church."
- Assign the remainder of chapter 11 of *Into All the World* and the book of Revelation. Ask participants to note items for discussion.

Session 14
- Allow time for discussion of questions raised by reading. The leader should be familiar with the major symbols of the book of Revelation (consult a Bible dictionary or a one-volume commentary), but cannot hope to know all of the details without exhaustive study. A better approach is to have the reference works on hand during the session in order to look up particular puzzles.
- Do the TRY THIS on page 146. Opinions may vary over who qualifies as an "oppressed Christian," but it would be best not to focus on that hassle. The heart of the matter is what the Gospel might say in addressing oppression wherever it is found. Allow about 30 minutes for the exercise.
- Invite individual(s) to use "Hope in the New Age" (Tape 4/Side B). This tape discusses both the apocalyptic hope in general and the book of Revelation's vision of the Holy City in particular.
- Assign pages 147-52 of *Into All the World* together with the three letters of John. Ask participants to note items for discussion.

Session 15
- Allow time for discussing questions raised by reading. Do not pass too quickly over the issue of authorship of the Johannine literature. There is a good summary of the problems connected with all of the Johannine writings in:
  Fuller, R.H., *The New Testament in Current Study.* pp. 101-32.
- Do the TRY THIS on page 151. Allow 30 minutes. If possible keep the discussion centered on the key issue: exclusivistic attitudes among Christians.
- Review with the participants the major themes of I John.
- Time might be taken for a discussion of textual variations such as that noted on page 151. Other examples of your own choosing may be cited and discussed. For those needing additional background on this subject the following will prove useful:
  Cambridge Bible Commentary (Introductory Volume). pp. 121-44
  OR
  The Interpreter's Bible (Vol. I). pp. 72-83
- Assign the remainder of chapter 12 of *Into All the World* together with the Gospel According to John. Ask participants to note items for discussion.

Session 16
- Allow time for discussion of questions raised by reading.
- Do the TRY THIS exercise on page 160. Few terms in Christian theology are more loaded with meaning than "eternal life," and you should have no trouble playing the word association game with it. Because of this, however, it may be very difficult for participants who have a long history with this word to move in the direction suggested. Be patient! Insight and discovery will be of more value here than rugged logic or abstraction.
- Wrap up loose ends of the entire study.
- Ask participants to bring reference works and tools to the final session.

Session 17
- Review the three Appendices and the use of each with the participants.
- Use the remainder of the Session for a full dress rehearsal of the ULTIMATE TRY THIS in Appendix III, using all the steps and appropriate tools. Your group can be broken into smaller units, each using one tool or contributing one step to the overall process. Using blackboards or large pieces of paper, let the smaller units report their findings to the larger group. Out of this should emerge a group effort at interpreting the Scriptures together.

The above schedule assumes 1½ hour sessions. Larger groups (15 or more) will find that group exercises and discussions take more time than is suggested above. Smaller groups (under 15) will find the suggestions about right.

ONE-HOUR SESSIONS
It is possible to adjust the above schedule to fit one-hour sessions in a variety of ways:
- Omit some of the inductive exercises
- Omit use of tape-recordings in class sessions
- Add additional sessions for chapters 3, 4, 7, 8, 9.
- Limit your group to 6–8 people

TWO-HOUR SESSIONS
It is possible to use the suggested breakdown of material in two-hour sessions by simply allowing more time for discussion of inductive exercises and/or of particular New Testament passages. Groups of 15 or more persons will find that the schedule outlined above requires at least two hours per session.

BREAKING UP THE STUDY
The proposed schedule of 17 plus sessions of 1½ hours each can be organized in a variety of ways. Many churches divide their adult study year into three terms: Fall, Winter, and Spring. Six to eight sessions each term can be used to break the study into three major sections:
  Fall: Acts and the Pauline Letters (chapters 1–5)
  Winter: The Synoptic Gospels (chapters 6–9)
  Spring: Post-Pauline Writings (chapters 10–12)
Using three terms such as this allows breathing time between the study of each New Testament section and thus avoids the confusion that can result from trying to do too much too quickly.

E. POSTSCRIPT

A part of our objective in developing this adult study was to aim for usability in a variety of local situations. Since no two groups are alike, nor the needs of any two churches, materials such as these require flexibility for use with different audiences. While these materials have already been used successfully in both large and small, rural and urban churches, past groups may not have anticipated the problems that can occur in their use with your group. Any suggestions, criticisms, creative adaptations, or particular problems encountered by new groups using *Into All the World* will be gratefully received by both the author and Griggs Educational Service. Our aim is to serve the needs of churches. Let us hear if we have hit the mark!